CW00420184

You Are Not Your Masks

YOU ARE NOT
YOUR MASKS

(PART 1)

A WAY OF LIBERATION & FINDING
FULFILMENT

SAIED SHAHSAVARI

You Are Not Your Masks

Copyrights Reserved © **2020** – Saied Shahsavari

ISBN: 9798696141688

No part of this book can be transmitted or reproduced in any form including print, electronic, photocopying, scanning, mechanical or recording without prior written permission from the author.

While the author has taken utmost efforts to ensure the accuracy of the written content, all readers are advised to follow the information mentioned herein at their own risk. This book has been written for information purposes only. Every effort has been made to make this book as complete and accurate as possible. However, there may be mistakes in typography or content. The purpose of this book is to educate.

DISCLAIMER

This book should be read as a manual for personal development. It is not intended to take the place of any professional medical or psychological opinion, and anyone who suffers from a mental or emotional condition should consult with relevant health professionals.

DEDICATIONS

To all my readers who find themselves in this book;

and in whose masks

I lose myself.

CONTENTS

Contents

PREFACE

For over 40 years, I have had the privilege of treating patients, travelling much of the world, and observing and helping people with a range of physical, mental, emotional, and spiritual problems. I am not an academic or a philosopher, nor am I a leader or follower of any religious group, but I have had the benefit of research, training, and contemplation.

Of course, what I am about to offer to you is not my discovery. In the past, many people from Buddha and Lao Tzu to Krishnamurti and Alan Watts have explained it in so many ways, either directly or indirectly, and in different languages. Yet, people still avoid looking at the fundamental roots of their problems, and instead try to sort out the superficial symptoms. My part is to simply clarify those problems and share the solutions that I have found in an understandable, doable, and achievable way.

In this book, I will discuss some simpler ways to find and sort out the roots of problems as opposed to dealing with just the symptoms and 'branches'. I don't want to give my readers vague or incompetent answers, but instead, I would like to offer smart questions and encourage readers to find answers for themselves. Having said that, I will also share some of the answers that other people, including myself, have found to work.

I have tried to transform very ancient eastern knowledge and complex spiritual ideas into modern, simple, and practical wisdom that people can use for themselves without the supervision of a guru or a master. There are a number of philosophies, ideologies, and opinions that try to show people a way of being such as Taoism, Buddhism, and Zen, but people of the 21st century have no time to go to temples and stay with masters for many years. My approach is to try to bring those temples to you, with an easy to understand formula so that you can experiment without having to sacrifice anything.

This book is intended as a manual for improving the quality of everyday life for everyone regardless of gender, cultural background, or religion. It is for those who are tired of trying endless ways to develop themselves with goal setting, relaxation, or meditation techniques, and are still failing to find their way and inner peace. Although this book is a self-help book for personal development, I would also like to think that it can help mental health professionals who want to try new ways and methods to treat their patients.

Please bear in mind that I am not saying this is 'the' way of liberation; it is one of the ways of liberation that I am sharing with you based on my understanding, professional career, and observation. If you try it and it works, it will become your way of freedom; but if it doesn't, it will remain as mine.

1

SELF-DEVELOPMENT: REALITY, MYTH, OR NECESSITY?

In most countries and cultures, there have always been two kinds of people. Those who live life as it has been given to them; that is to say they breathe, they eat, and they push through one day into the next until they finally reach the end. Then there are others who wish to explore, in terms of exploring the meaning and purpose of life. These people isolated themselves from others and lived life as monks or spent time in temples in search of answers. This process of self-exploration not only helped them acquire a purpose but also healed them in many ways. People who chose to explore life found meaning and true happiness.

The first kind who spent life barely living are known as 'modern people': people following a basic robotic routine that involves eating, working, sleeping, and repeating the same actions all over again. However, every decision we make and action we take is because somewhere in our subconscious mind, we long for true happiness and well-being.

The problem lies in where we think true happiness is, and what we think our well-being depends on. Over time, the world has shifted its priorities to money and lifestyle. This has caused many of us to perceive happiness as something that can be achieved through materialistic things. The reality is quite the opposite. Moreover, when we realise that we aren't well or happy, we look for answers in other ways, such as prescribed or unprescribed drugs and connections with friends.

There is so much information out there on why you need to develop yourself, but so little on how to do this simply. The self-help industry, while it talks much about the formulas of self-development, also tends to overlook the essential lessons and personal methods needed for living a better life. This is exactly why so many people follow common advice and misconceptions and find themselves with short-lived results.

It is important to note that the changes over the past few years have presented many challenges to the generation of the 21st century— particularly the constant pressure to excel in a technological age. The pain and pressure of bettering one's self has caused much mental distress, and mental illness is a growing global concern. In 2018, over 6,500 suicides were recorded in the UK alone.

The need for real happiness based on well-being has to be seen as a priority and necessity for everyone, now. If this generation is the most comfortable, in all countries all around the world, why then is mental health one of the most difficult problems that societies face? This raises a fundamental question: is it a great society that makes happy and great people, or is it happy, calm, and creative people that make a society great, or both?

It is obvious that at some stage, our attention and focus shifted to creating a comfortable society, and we truly forgot how to teach and help people with their self-development. We teach our children everything they need from mathematics to art, but nothing about self-development technology, which would enable them to live happier, calmer, and more harmonious lives within society and the world they live in. When it comes to developing cars or buildings, for instance, we teach them all the necessary knowledge and skills, but when it comes to self-discovery and personal development, we expect them to figure things out by themselves!

Educational institutions have prepared people for navigating and exploring the materialistic world, but never for self-exploration. This basic mistake has led people to believing their happiness and well-being lies in things, events, and lifestyle. The importance of self-discovery and personal development goes unnoticed. We often brush off our shortcomings and refuse to find and accept the fundamental reasons for our problems. We wilfully ignore our failings in the pursuit of temporary happiness.

However, in the long-term, the negative impact of avoiding our issues reveals itself in many aspects of our lives. When we place our happiness in man-made things, we do not realise it is just temptation: a feeling that will fade away with time and make us feel the same way we did in the beginning. Hence, the statistic of people with mental and emotional illnesses and disorders shows how many people are struggling to figure out what to do with themselves, and the number of suicides shows how many of them have given up. Teenagers and young adults are engulfed by more problems than ever before. They are more worried about what is expected of them rather than discovering what is true about themselves. They continue to follow the social standards of today and display behaviours that indicate failure, impatience, and irresponsibility.

Self-improvement and personal development are just as important as academic learning. In fact, finding ourselves is far more important than finding the 'x' in algebra. We need to be more aware, more accepting, and more adaptable in our lives in order to consciously bring changes in our mind. If we are not going to self-observe and analyse our responses to different things in life, we will continue to push our happiness further away.

Therefore, in my opinion, we need to work together, with open minds, to develop a reliable and simple system that is focused on helping individuals find, know, and develop themselves naturally and harmoniously. If we can achieve this, we can build a better society in which everyone can discover their true potential – and in this way, we'll stem the growing psychological crisis of today.

You may wonder why it should be simple. Why look for easier ways when we can implement the ways we already have? The thing is, the current generation has been overfed with instant gratification. Long gone are the days when hard work was trending. In today's world, hard work is still appreciated, but smart work is preferred. Besides, we may often think of shutting out our daily lives and driving off to somewhere remote. But can we really? The truth is, while our mind and body do need rest, peace, and true happiness, the way we believe we can achieve it is not practical in this century anymore. Hence, a lot of us may not know it, but we are in desperate need of simpler ways to rest our minds and bodies now.

Just as we continue to learn academically, our self-discovery and self-development journey should also continue. We should be focused on continuous self-development regardless of what phase of life we are in. We must self-educate by consciously directing our responsibility so that we can develop an innate quality or personality that is balanced, knowledgeable, and skilled. Moreover, we need to initiate self-growth to develop optimal qualities and abilities in order to fulfil our most important needs: mental, emotional, and perceptual, to improve each phase of our lives.

As you live each day, you will inevitably face different situations and be required to adapt to different roles. When you self-observe and become more aware, you will notice that you tend to live past the masks of your life and act in harmony with who you really are. Even if you do not find success in every mask or role and responsibility, you will still find each experience more fulfilling. When your qualities and values are synchronised with your objectives, you will not wait for good things to happen – instead you will focus on how you can create the outcomes of your choices.

Being self-aware will also help you find your own innate qualities and personal methods, and from this, you will be able to identify what works for you and what doesn't. You will focus on the bigger picture and be able to determine what makes a situation better or worse. Where does this problem stem from? Which personal method can I apply to solve this problem? Questions like these will urge you to search for the fundamental roots of the challenges and problems you face in your life. Remember: when you do not want something to grow, you do not cut its stem, you pull it out at the root.

2

BACK TO BASICS

There are many things that I have not personally experienced in my life, and there are so many questions about life that I have no answers to, but I can share my knowledge of mental and emotional health and self-development without claiming that what I say is the only truth. I also would like to assure you of my honesty about everything I will be sharing with you, because all of the points that I make in this book are based on the best of my knowledge and experience so far. I might find in the future that I may experience new things or come across different ideas that complement my current view or change it completely. So, what I am offering you now is not absolute or final. You and I both can change it dynamically based on our own knowledge, experiences, and feelings in the present moment. The point is, knowledge is never-ending, and we can never consume all of it. There is always going to be something new to learn and more information to add, and my ideas are completely open to it.

What I would like to do is simplify the basic aspects of life that have become overly complicated and mysterious in people's minds over the years. That same complexity forms the foundation and root of most of the mental, emotional, and even physical disorders and diseases we face.

If we wanted to understand and analyse a building, we shouldn't start from the fourth or fifth floor. We need to examine the foundation of the building and its stability and quality first, and then analyse the rest of the floors. Likewise, with our mental illnesses, we cannot start from the symptoms without considering the roots and identifying the causes. Even though, in almost all cases, the sufferers themselves don't know the origin of their problems and only complain about the symptoms.

It is obvious that if we categorise a problem as purely physical, we expect a physician to deal with it. Likewise, we expect that mental illnesses and emotional problems should be dealt with by psychiatrists and psychologists, in the same way that a plumber deals with a plumbing problem and builders deal with building problems. Therefore, when people and the government both say that the number one problem in society is mental diseases and disorders, it is logical to expect psychiatrists and psychologists to deal with the problem. But despite these dedicated professionals trying their best, the statistics in recent decades show that mental health issues are much worse than before.

It is incredibly concerning to see the increase in mental illness and suicide rates, especially in young people. And in 2020, mental health issues are likely to be much worse worldwide due to stress caused by the Covid-19 pandemic, including isolation, bereavement, loss of employment, financial difficulties, domestic violence, and so on. This leaves us with many more concerns and questions than experts.

If we look at the roots of mental and emotional illnesses and disorders holistically, could we seek help from all the professionals whose work somehow relates to different aspects of our lives? It is my opinion that if we want to tackle society's main mental and emotional issues, everyone including parents, children, teachers, healthcare practitioners, the government, the police, and anyone who works with people — even bus drivers — needs to help one another under one umbrella (of course within their allowed field). Each of us has a role to play; we must all be in this together.

If, for example, a lady who suffers from anxiety doesn't feel well when she runs for a bus in the morning, couldn't the smile of a friendly bus driver help to reduce her stress and anxiety? When it comes to mental illness, every little help helps. So, based on these ideas, shopkeepers, cleaners, dieticians, solicitors, civil enforcement officers, and everyone else, with simple training, can help reduce people's mental pressure, provided that they do not interfere or offer advice. Obviously, if you feel well in your own mind, your attitude towards others will improve. So, the first thing that people can do to help society is to start with their own self-help programme.

In this book, I will discuss the roots of the common problems I have seen in my patients and others over the years, and the ways in which you can help yourself and others. As I have mentioned, this book is not a substitute for any medical treatment, and the main purpose is to share my knowledge with you and also to ask you to consider the roots of the problems you identify with in your own life.

I have full respect for other professionals in different fields who are trying their best to help society, to prevent mental disorders or cure them by providing medical treatments, writing books, running workshops and teaching, etc. My own ideas and approaches may differ from others but in no way discredits them. It is my obligation to contribute to the world I live in and do my part in helping people who need support by offering new ways of looking at self-development issues. The only rule knowledge brings with it is to spread it further, and that is exactly what I intend on doing.

3

THE SECRET OF OUR EXISTENCE

Following my very important principle for this book — the basics — I would like to start from the foundation of my ideas and the root of all mental and emotional illnesses and disorders. In order to simplify this, I will share with you a fundamental secret of our existence.

The world of 'being' and the world of 'doing' are concentric circles; we live in two different yet united worlds. The circle with infinite circumference is our being, which most of us are not familiar with. The world of doing is what we refer to and know as our life, the real world, and our existence.

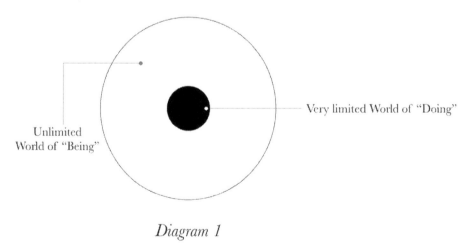

Diagram 1

The World of Doing

The world of doing is like a big stage for the performance of our daily lives. Imagine this stage is inside a prison. Since you were born inside this prison, it is very obvious that you don't know about it, and you also have no idea or concept of the world outside of this prison. All of our daily lives, the rules, and other important or unimportant aspects of our lives are happening on this stage inside the prison. Our knowledge and understanding of ourselves, the people around us, and the whole world around us takes place on this stage too. There is nothing you can remember, imagine, or do outside of this stage.

This little world of doing has rules that all of us should pay attention to in order to play well and exist on this stage. We all need at least one mask to qualify to play a character on this stage, and it starts when we accept our first mask from our parents or guardians. The first mask qualifies us to enter and perform on the stage of the world of doing. Then, in order to continue our performances, we need some other masks such as that of a brother or sister, a friend, a citizen, and so on.

Masks need memories to survive and perform. So, for a mask, the power of recording incidents and recalling them is essential for them to act and perform consistently. The world of doing requires the power of memory for you to accept your mask and allow you to continue to survive. For example, as a child, you need to understand that you are the son or daughter of your parents, and you have to remember, follow, and trust them for your survival and growth.

Our memory needs to use our five senses in the field of time because time is an imaginary platform for memory, and without it, memory cannot carry on. So, taking a simple example: you put a mask on and become a driver. Then, you sit in your car, which is your memory, and drive on a one-way road, which is time. Your life in your mind becomes divided into three different parts: the past (what you see in your rear-view mirror), the present (what exists on the sides of your car and what is in your windscreen), and the future (what you imagine and expect to see later). Using time as a platform is the only way memory can continuously help your different masks operate by pretending that the past and the future exist. However, in reality, only the present time (if you still call it time) exists, and the past and the future are an illusion based on your memory and imagination.

Time gives us the illusion of the past and the future, and based on those, we start to think. Memory is based on the past and the imagination of the future, which is mainly based on the past, too. For example: if you didn't know what an island was, but I asked if you knew the meaning of land and water, and you did (based on your memory), then I could ask you to use your imagination and imagine a piece of land surrounded by water. In this example, you can see how the past is so important: not only in the way of using your memory, but it also gives you a foundation to use your imagination and the future. How useless then is the present time in your daily life?

Please understand, I am not against memory or imagination. On the contrary, I respect them both as they are two of the most useful and amazing features of consciousness. All science, philosophy, history, mathematics, literature, language, and whatever you find in libraries and in our civilisation as a whole are mainly the result of memory and imagination. Our entire education is based on studying mankind's achievements in the past, coupled with the imagination to design new things.

As you can see, the present is useless in this process. It is as narrow as a little bridge of one second to the next between the hugely important past and future. That is the reason why, when some people get dementia (and lose their memories), all of their daily life abilities, knowledge, qualifications, experiences, and even their personalities disappear.

Therefore, masks are mainly based on the past and slightly on the future, and what you call your mind is just gathered data from the past with some imagination and expectation based on patterns from your past, projected to the future. That is exactly why minds always either go back to the past or to the future, while staying in the present time and now is very difficult.

If you were to look at your life, you would realise that the present is the most useless part of your time. Even on your watch, the present second is just a very tiny little bridge between the past and the future. You can remember the past and use it as a powerful platform to predict, imagine, or design your future, but what are you going to do with the present? Everything you see will be judged and understood based on your knowledge and experience of the past. When you say you don't understand something, it means you can't find any reference for it in your personal experience, or from the data that you have gathered, or in the science you have learnt that is stored in the past section of your mind.

My interest is not to prove these points as philosophical ideas or theories, as they've already been mentioned by so many people in so many ways. I am interested in showing you the practical side of understanding and feeling these points so that they can enable you to work with your masks much more efficiently. I will later explain how these imaginary concepts can cause the most severe mental disorders: depression (caused by the past) and anxiety (caused by the future).

The World of Being

There is no satisfactory way to use either verbal or written words that were created in the world of doing to explain or describe the world of being.

The world of being is about existence in the core, with no need for explanation, description, languages, or names. This is well explained by Master Lao Tzu as Tao in the first chapter of *Tao Te Ching*.

A baby exists outside of time or thinking, with no memory or imagination, and he or she responds to real stimulants, pleasant or painful touch, and basic needs such as hunger and thirst. If we ask why they have no memory or imagination, it is simply because babies have no masks given to them, and they don't need a mask to stay alive. By accepting their first mask, their memory starts to work, and needs time to function. As his or her mind starts to exist and gradually grow, they forget about the world of existence. I would suggest we change the word 'human being' to 'human doing' as people are much more interested in doing. Even when they see each other, instead of asking, "how are you?" people commonly ask, "how are you doing?"

The world of being can be felt when you unplug from all of your masks and become one. You become one when you stop talking to yourself and meditation happens. Meditation is not something you do. It is the state of your awareness when you stop doing anything. Relaxation is for the world of doing, to reduce the pressure of life, enhance performance, lessen stress and anxiety, and improve focus and memory. Meditation, however, is the gate to feeling being.

What can we say about the world of being when language has been developed in the world of doing? Language facilitates verbal and written communication between members of the world of doing who either live at the same time or in a different historical time.

If you manage to grow enough to improve the state of your consciousness, you might be able to feel the world of being, but there is nothing you can do directly to get this feeling. However, whatever you do in the world of doing is part of the world of being, too.

As I said at the beginning of this chapter, I am not trying to explain the world of being as it is impossible. But hopefully by the end of this book, you will all have some idea about the preparation and special relaxation needed to feel your real existence without requiring any background.

Since I don't want you to look at this as a philosophical idea, I would suggest that you don't think about it too much at this stage. Come back to this chapter and read it again after you have finished the book.

4

THE WORLD OF DOING AND THE FIVE SENSES

If you used five lines to symbolise the five senses, and you draw them in a way that they meet one another in the centre, you would create a circle that represents your world of doing.

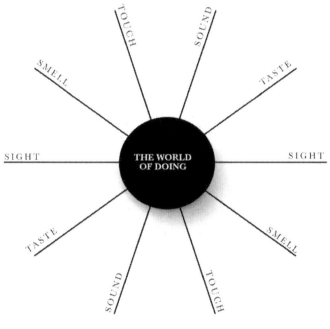

Diagram 2

What you call your 'world' is actually the common point between all of your five senses: vision, hearing, smell, touch, and taste – and also your mental perception, which is based on the past. You can make the lines weaker or stronger, which will ultimately change the size and the quality of your world. This circle is only based on one direction that works from the inside out, bringing back some information from the outside world.

Your five senses are needed to survive in the world of doing. You obtain data and information that you need to act and react to outside stimulants. For example, if you saw a tiger and heard it coming towards you, you would immediately recognise it as a dangerous animal and run to safety. What people call reality is based on the combination of all five senses. The more the five senses are involved, the more you will perceive your experience to be real. Those who were not gifted senses like vision or hearing will perceive reality differently.

In the world of doing, the five senses need space and the illusion of time to operate. They work based on registering resistance and reflections of different objects by your natural organs; for example, your eyes register the resistance of any object against light, and your ears register sound against your eardrums.

If there is no resistance to light, you won't be able to see different objects around you. It is more or less the same with other senses and the way they operate. For example, your touch registers the resistance of an object against the movement of your hand.

However, it is important for you to know that the five senses can also be used for feeling and realising the world of being, provided you use them in both directions (forward and backward), which can help you feel the different dimensions of life. Alan Watts used the example of the headlights on your car. They can be used outwardly to see what is in front of your car, but they cannot be used to see or be aware of the engine behind them, which is the source of power.

What all major spiritual leaders such as Lao Tzu have tried to suggest is that by using your senses backwards, you become aware of the source of your consciousness.

This simple technique is so difficult to explain to those who have always lived, and have been trapped, in the world of doing. Therefore, I mention it only briefly here and will take this forward in simple ways throughout the book so that you can familiarise yourself with the concept and absorb it gradually.

5

WHAT YOU KNOW AS SELF: THE COMMON AREAS OF MASKS

It is so important to understand what you mean exactly when you refer to the word 'I'? If 'I' is a circle, how wide is its circumference? I am not asking this to check your knowledge and what you have learnt from others and books. I am asking you a simple, direct question, so you can examine your own feeling of the 'self.'

By using the word 'I', are you referring to your body or mind, or perhaps referring to the personal conversation with yourself in your mind? If a surgeon were to open your abdomen, for example, would you look at your organs as a place of your 'I', or still look into them from the outside?

When you visit a psychologist or doctor and say, "I suffer from this or that problem…I believe in this or that idea…I am like this and not like that…I love this…I hate that," where is your 'I' exactly, and who is talking about you using your mouth?

When you talk about your shoes, for example, that means you and your shoes are two different existences, and that enables you to comment about your shoes. In the same way, when you talk about yourself, you become two separate existences; one is the person who is talking, and the other one is whom the comment is about. Which one of the above are you? And which one do you refer to as your real self or 'I'?

Is your mind or soul inside of your brain and your body, or is it the other way around, and your physical body is inside of your mind or soul? How much, inclusively or exclusively, do you feel as 'I'? What parts of your daily life are within your feeling of 'I'? Obviously, your therapist starts by listening to you and tries to explain to you that 'you' suffer from this or that problem, but my approach is much deeper than that. It asks you who is suffering, and the basic question is: who is your 'I' and what is the relationship between you and the reporter in your mind who is using your mouth to talk about you? For example, if you tell your therapist, "My friend Jack is suffering from mental and emotional problems," that means your friend Jack is the subject of your report, and you are the reporter. When you say 'I' suffer from these problems, who is the subject, and who is the reporter? Which one are you? If you try to answer that you are both the subject and the reporter, then who is the third one talking about the other two? If you use this approach to think, you will carry on until you have thousands of 'I's'.

It is also the same when people say that they want to improve themselves because they are lazy, depressed, anxious, or stressed. But how are they going to do it? You can go to the gym to improve your physical power and lift heavy weights, but can you go to the gym and lift yourself off the floor in one day? It is as impossible as they say, as "pulling oneself up by one's bootstraps".

This is also the main reason why religious morality, and mental and emotional solutions, do not work long-term or address the root of one's problems. The proof of this, as I have said, is the growing number of mental health diseases and disorders around the world.

Since I have promised to simplify everything I can, let me explain to you who is your 'I' in a very simple way. When you accept different masks from your family, friends, colleagues, community, and so on, all of these masks have one little point in common and work with your memory. It is this little part that you call 'I', which has nothing to do with your existence. It is obvious that in order to perform in the world of doing, you need all these masks, but they are not all equally important and they don't work the same way.

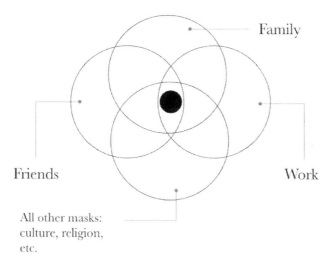

Diagram 3

Your existence is your vibration, which is related to the whole network of the universe and its border. It very much depends on your feeling of life in general and your life individually. To show you what I really mean when I talk about the common areas between your masks, I have illustrated this concept in a diagram. The number and size of the circles, in reality, varies between people. For some of you, the family circle might be the largest circle, whereas for others, it might be work. Yet the common area between the circles remains the same. I/Self/Me/Ego/Sense of Existence are all names for the common area between all of the masks we need and have in order to take part in the world of doing.

This also explains that the idea of self-improvement or self-development is nonsense and imaginary. How can you improve yourself when you are trapped between the circles of your masks? No matter how many times you set goals and try your best, you won't be able to do it because you are living in these roles and masks. You cannot decide to get rid of masks or improve them. Rules, philosophies, ideologies, and morality can partly help you get what you want, but because the masks need to use force, your existence will soon start to resist, which explains how, for example, a priest who abstains from physical pleasure and marriage becomes a paedophile or commits sexual assault against children.

That is why when you ask a question from a Zen master or a guru, they try to help you feel 'I' by asking you who is asking that question. They try to point out that you, as one separate existence that can have a problem or a question, do not exist. 'I' is just an idea that happens only in the moment you stop growing. It is very useful for social convenience and working with others in the world of doing, but you shouldn't take it seriously and accept it as part of your real existence.

I will explain in later chapters how you can feel your existence behind your masks, and as you do that, you will see a lot of changes transpire within you and in your life as the result of your realisation. These changes will not just be plans and programmes you can do or practise to get better; these changes will push you to achieve self-fulfilment and greatness on another level.

6

RULES OF MASKS

Masks possess their own specific rules; however, if we do not pay attention to these rules, we will not be able to become aware of our existence behind our masks. Simply put, awareness and growth do not take place if we don't find out the rules of our masks and how to use them smartly.

So many amazing masters including Lao Tzu and Buddha have mentioned the rules of masks in so many different ways. For years, I have been personally contemplating, observing, experimenting, learning, reading, and practising many forms of inner investigation to find out more about the rules of masks. However, I still cannot claim that I have found all of the rules. As this is a fundamental rule of the world of doing, I would like to encourage you to try and find the rules of your own masks. Pay attention to yourself, observe, and re-evaluate. The journey of self-discovery is not going to be you by yourself. I, too, will share some of my findings with you in great hope that you will also add yours into my simple list through your own contemplation and inner investigations.

As I mentioned, we all need at least one mask to be able to perform in the world of doing. We all start with the first mask and then increase the number and quality of the masks we need. Over 40 years, I have observed myself, family and friends, many masters, and patients to find out more about the rules of masks.

When you find out about the rules of your masks and stop identifying and associating yourself with any of them, you will be able to do four important things with your masks. I am going to explain to you in simple terms how you can use these in your personal lives.

a. Recognise your negative, unwanted, and useless masks, and get rid of them. There are so many negative masks that you may be unwillingly using when they should actually be discarded. Or, if you can't discard those masks, you can minimise them to become an insignificant part of your life. For example, if you have a friend who encourages you to do drugs, you can avoid them and directly let them know you do not want to be their friend anymore and give them their mask back. If a negative mask comes from one of your family members like your parents, you won't be able to discard it, but you can reduce its influence on you by making it as weak as possible. Often, we attach ourselves to people who are toxic, and we may not realise it at first, but their presence absorbs our vital energy and reduces our chance of growing. Once we realise we are associated with such masks, it is time to let go.

b. Masks that are positive and helpful in your life can be constantly improved upon, and you can use your creativity to progress them in any direction you want. For example, if you are a teacher and you love your job, you can constantly improve your communication skills, techniques, and connection with your students, and it will help you and your students in so many unimaginable ways. Another example might be if you are friends with someone who has a healthy attitude to life and encourages you to practise relaxation methods every day. You might want to keep that mask and consider their advice.

c. By understanding the rules of your masks, you can also create the masks you need. Generally, as I have mentioned, your masks are provided by others – that is why you will always need those who gave you your masks to confirm, renew, and update them, especially the positive ones. The main cause of psychological neediness comes from this very foundation. For example, we often see that couples need to remind each other that they love one another, and we see it in children who need to be the centre of their parent's attention. It is important that we understand that this can also create the wrong result, and we will return to this idea later on.

d. Lastly, and most importantly, by using the knowledge of your masks and also some relaxation methods, you can be ready to move behind all of your masks and feel your total freedom or meditation. At this stage, you will have a good level of control over your life in the world of doing, and also feel your existence in the world of being.

Your masks are split into categories ranging from level 1 to the nth level. Every single person, based on their upbringing, mental progression, and education, has unique ways of organising their masks into levels. For example, some people keep only one mask in level 1, while others have more, and so on.

Generally, the first few levels of masks (but especially level 1) describe our personality and ego. This is why really understanding the level 1 mask(s) in your life will help you to get closer to your self-discovery and growth. Being aware of level 1 masks also makes it easier for you to prevent all sorts of mental and emotional issues. The majority of mental disorders are hidden with no obvious symptoms for a long time, and people suffer from them without knowing the cause. In my professional life, I have seen so many cases of parents who desperately wanted to help their children who were suffering from mental issues, but didn't realise that *they* were, in fact, the root of their children's problems.

The difficulty in discarding, improving, or creating any of your masks starts from level 1. However, once you have passed this level, it does, in fact, make the others easier. Understanding the levels of masks and their interrelated nature helps us understand the roots of so many physical and mental problems related to the world of doing.

7

THE LEVELS OF MASKS

As explained, there are two worlds: the world of doing and the world of being. When man comes into this world, he does not understand, does not think, and does not remember. Thus, he is in the world of being.

Gradually, when he grows up a little, he grabs on to his first mask as a child, and that first mask begins from level 1 as the highest level.

Level 1

Practically, it is common for an individual to have their first mask identifying as a child, and then transition into other roles in life. The first mask only comes from their parents, specifically from mothers. You have to realise that this mask stays relevant and important for as long as there aren't any other masks or roles to replace it. In level 1, an individual's first mask remains the most important until they transition into adulthood and decide to either add or replace this mask with the mask they receive from people they love, typically a husband/wife or partner.

As an individual grows up with this mask, they invariably experience many changes that reshape their lives for the foreseeable future. That is why level 1 masks are so important – they give people their main characters and roles and, in most cases, influence their beliefs, emotions, or ego. It is also often within this level that people develop other important aspects of their lives, including their culture, religion, ideology, and personal beliefs.

However, as people move forward and accept other masks along the way, they begin to act and react in a certain way. This is because we accept the fact that we have stepped into the world of doing. When we step into the world of doing, it is inevitable for us to have problems, especially the psychological and emotional kind. It is commonly, but not always, the case that when we dive into the depths of the mess that our minds have created, we are often met with something that relates to level 1. That being said, it is important to state that these problems are not necessarily caused by the masks at level 1. They can also be a result of misinformation, attitude, perception, the wrong mask, or just misunderstanding.

As we experience a high degree of change and learning in life, all of our emotional and mental changes transpire at this level. This presents us with an opportunity to find the answers to some of the main questions about our mental and emotional states. Most of our mental and emotional changes, deficiencies, successes, or problems emanate from level 1 masks.

As each individual is different, everyone has their own logic. Yet despite the differences and differing perspectives of one's own life experiences compared to another's, the root of all personal logic usually comes from level 1 masks. Occasionally you find that it comes from a combination of masks from different levels. Again, the reasons for which can differ.

The foundation for the roots of ego and communication are also based on masks from level one. If masks from level 2 disappear, or we have problems with them, we can always go back to level 1 for help or comfort. But if the masks from level 1 disappear or cause trouble, there's really no other level to go back to. This is why people created God(s) to turn to, or other spiritual doors to deal with their grief from level 1. In the world of doing, there is no place higher than level 1.

The masks of level 1 are the foundation of who you were, who you are, and who you might become. They will always remain inside of you regardless of how many levels you add on. However, if you lose the masks from level 1, life still isn't over. It will be different, and it might take time and effort to deal with the huge change in your world of doing, but things will settle down. Although there is no point in going from level 1 to level 2, the masks of level 2 might still play their role in dealing with the disappearance of the masks of level 1. How does that work? Let's see.

Level 2

As we grow up, we begin to accept more masks. Level 2 is quite close to level 1. This is why the masks of level 2 are often promoted to level 1. Level 2 masks are added when you delve into completely different roles beyond your role of being someone's son or daughter. While these masks are very important, they still aren't as important as level 1. You may find yourself sacrificing your life to protect level 1 masks, but not level 2. They are added to your package; some are based on your choices mainly as you grow up, such as school friends. The most important thing to understand and remember about the masks of level 2 is that they are the most important ones after level 1.

You may also find yourself changing these masks as your choices and needs change over time. For instance, you may change your job role, and progress from being a team member to a manager, and hence, change your mask to fit your new responsibilities. In addition, masks from level 2 usually complement one or some of the masks from level 1. For example, imagine that your father always wanted you to become a doctor, and you chose medicine as your career, not because you love it but because you love your father and wanted to make him proud.

What happens then when your father passes away? Tolerating that job might become difficult, and you might look to replace your father's mask with the mask of someone else who is proud of you. Or you might find comfort in telling the story of how proud your father was of you in his memory.

Similarly, for example, your mother loves cats but you hate them. You only tolerate them because your mother wants to keep them. You often have fights over how the cats irritate you, but unfortunately, now your mother has passed away and all of a sudden you want to keep them. You want to feed them because you know your mother loved them and how much they meant to her. They no longer irritate you. This also tells us that the masks from any level can be promoted, given the circumstances or choices. Therefore, not all, but most level 2 masks are subsets of level 1 masks.

The most amazing characteristics of masks at different levels is their ability to be replaced or moved between levels. For instance, level 2 masks are highly likely to be promoted to level 1, but if this movement happens too quickly, it can cause confusion and emotional and mental distress. The promotion or demotion of masks should be gradual enough for the mind to accept and react accordingly.

Therefore, the masks of level 3 or 4 cannot jump straight to level 1. Similarly, demoting the masks of level 1 directly to level 3 or 4 might create problems later. Remember, it is a matter of emotions and priorities. Any instant alteration may result in inner chaos.

Imagine a scenario where you meet a person by chance at a bar. You talk for hours, and when you get home you feel like you're in love. Even if you are, it is really essential to take things slow. Usually, love doesn't come that easy, but who knows? Love is different for everyone. The point here is not to rush regardless, because if you jump a mask from level 4 or 5 to level 1, you might face some serious consequences.

If the person you have just met feels the same, and you agree on getting married, they ought to become your life partner, which puts them on level 1. However, it is usually the case that once you've got what you both wanted, it doesn't really seem like the fairytale you thought it would be, and this is because you rushed. Know that in the world of doing, patience and time is key. Everything has to have a proper timeline; every decision and act has to serve a proper time frame to avoid disturbances.

Now let's suppose this time you meet this person at a bar, and you feel like you love them, so you talk to them for days, and you get to know them and gradually promote them from a low level up to level 3. Eventually, you decide to express your love for them, and thankfully, they feel the same. You promote them to level 2. As we've already said, level 2 is the most important level after level 1. Finally, you decide to get married, and they get promoted to level 1. This gradual process is what helps bring emotional and psychological stability, which in turn supports the health of your relationships and life.

Problems arise in not understanding the levels of each mask and how they each require time, patience, and proper decision-making before promoting or demoting.

The influence of public figures on masks is also quite powerful and interesting. For example, if a celebrity or a football team you support suddenly encourages violence or some sort of protest, you will automatically be inclined towards the thought of it, if it's in level 2. Since the decision is completely in your hands, you might just be emotionally aggravated enough to promote them to level 1. This will then make you become a part of those protests. My point here is that there is a thin line between level 1 and level 2, and being able to differentiate them both is highly important.

The influence of high-level mask providers can also be used to positively demote others' masks. For instance, you might have a friend who is a drug addict, and you tell them that if they don't go to rehab they might lose your friendship. Now, because you are on level 1, the influence you have might be powerful. This could help them demote their drug addiction to lower levels and one day be free from drug addiction.

The key is in knowing the masks of each level, and the lines between them.

Level 3 and below

As we grow in life, there may be times where we have to give priority to the masks on level 3. For example, your boss asks you to change your shift patterns for months, and they do not align with your family hours. Your family disapproves, but you have to agree with your boss as it is an order and you need to earn money for your family. Now, this may be a decision from the masks of level 3, but it is still influenced by level 1.

Masks in level 3 and below exist, and they are also useful. Your colleagues, neighbours, and other things associated with you are under the umbrella of level 3 masks. We may or may not emotionally attach ourselves to these masks/roles, but they are important for society and your own personal development.

You may ask why there is a need to pay attention to levels 2, 3, and below if they are not as important as level 1. The reason we need to pay attention to them is that they help us act in certain roles and in some of the masks we may promote their levels in our minds. For example, when you are representing a level 3 mask such as a colleague, it may not be that important; however, if you become friends with them, your mask moves to a higher level. If one day you fall in love with one of them, they move to the highest level — level 1 — along with the people that you see as the most important in your life. In short, these masks grow in importance as you move forward and involve yourself more in the world of doing. Now that you know how to identify the roles and masks in your life, you can contemplate and find lots of your masks at different levels. Study their importance and reasons for existence.

As I have mentioned, your masks also come in packages, and you cannot accept and use only one part of them – you have to be aware of the use of each mask in different levels. In the short term, you may be able to avoid some parts of their packages but, very soon, they will reach you and force you to start to use the whole package. For example, you may say that you love a drug addict, but you don't do drugs and you don't mind if they do. However, if you continue to use the mask you have accepted from them, the other aspects of the package will catch up with you, and you may also become a drug addict. There are several stories in the public domain that illustrate this point, but the key message is that you cannot pick a part of a mask and ignore the package that comes with it.

There are ways in which unimportant masks in people's lives move to higher or lower levels and end up influencing their lifestyle. We can find many examples of this in the stories of celebrities who have tried to pick a part of the masks that they use in their lives, but the rest of the packages eventually surfaced and caught up with them later on.

This brings us to realise why we need to be consciously aware of our masks and their levels, and how they can be influenced or change through someone else's masks' influence. You can't avoid your identity masks and the roles they play in your life for a long period of time. You have to consciously study their existence and purpose. However, one of the most complex things that philosophers and psychologists have had to face is their difficulty explaining the differences between consciousness and ego. Most people hold onto their masks, not giving themselves room to qualify for masks of higher levels, which is why we need to understand how we can differentiate between these two phenomena and understand why we need to be more conscious and less egotistic.

Here's an unusual example to explain an important point. Your hands are useful because you can grab things, but that isn't the whole story. You can also let things go. Imagine waking up one day to find your hands are sticky. You can grab things, but you aren't able to let things go. Are they useful now? As a matter of fact, no! Instead, they are a source of mess and panic. You cannot move on in life with things like your toothbrush or your hairbrush or anything else attached to your hands, can you? These things may be important for a minute in your daily life, but you cannot continue your day effectively without letting them go.

Similarly, consciousness, in the world of doing, needs to connect to different aspects of your life either through your memory or imagination. But if you use glue and rigidly stick to things in your memory or imagination, then your life is likely to become difficult and perhaps even unbearable.

Consciousness with glue is ego. Ego is gluey, and it can stick to different aspects of your life both from the past and the future. When your ego stubbornly sticks to your past, it causes depression; when it sticks to the future, it causes anxiety; and when it sticks to both, you find yourself suffering from a mixture of depression and anxiety.

Since the past and the future are both imaginary and do not exist, depression and anxiety also do not exist. Only those who stick very strongly to this gluey ego, both in the past and future, suffer from these imaginary problems. So, if you try to solve depression or anxiety without addressing and solving the glue of your ego, you will find yourself beating the air and throwing water into the sea! It is one of the main reasons some people who suffer from too much glue need distractions, such as alcohol and drugs, to reduce the power of their sticky memory and imagination. It is one reason why the power of attaching and detaching to anything and everything in your life makes you immune to most of the psychological and emotional diseases and disorders.

Hence, the ideology with masks is that they're important but need to be prioritised only when needed. You cannot obsess over a mask and expect to live the rest of your life easily.cles will eventually arise, and that is not something any of us wants.

8

MEDITATION, RELAXATION, AND MASKS

For years, I've been explaining what meditation really is and how one can actually feel it. In the past, in eastern cultures, meditation has been introduced to man in various forms and terms. However, over time it has lost its essence and become trapped in different meanings and purposes.

Before we dive into the depths of meditation, I would like to highlight the intention of this chapter. It is not to discredit anyone's idea, theory, or understanding of meditation, but rather to propose a new way for you to approach and understand it. In short, it is my point of view.

Since meditation was discovered, the world has produced various books, classes, and other sources of information on its benefits. However, a lot of people have asked me whether it really works because the results they achieved weren't what they expected. In the worst cases, people ended up experiencing physical pain in their knees, back, and joints.

It is undeniable that people have always found some benefit in practicing what they have been introduced to as meditation. But my point is that those benefits were not the result of meditation. Benefits are the result of doing the right acts at the right time, and mediation is not about doing. In fact, it is the complete opposite. In order to meditate, one needs to completely stop doing anything and everything. When you 'do' something, you will have likely learnt it from someone else who knows more than you. You will have memorised the techniques and practiced doing it correctly to get a desirable result. Meditation has no benefit and no techniques to practice!

I can see the root of the confusion surrounding meditation and the reasons for so many people's fruitless searches and lack of results. But I would like to emphasise again that I do not want to criticise or blame any meditation systems, teachers, books, or other sources for the confusion, as they have tried their best to help people who were seeking real calmness and enlightenment. I just want to share my opinion and findings on meditation and offer it as *a* way and *another* approach to awakening, as opposed to claiming it is *the* way.

When you learn meditation or apply its 'technique' you're actually working your way towards meditation. Meditation itself is where you stop working or even thinking for that matter. Meditation is an act of realisation. It is an act of being, and it exists in the world of being rather than in the world of doing.

When you google "what is meditation?" over 489 million websites appear with various definitions, but I have always struggled to define meditation and explain it. That is because meditation is the first entry point into the world of being where all the tools of the world of doing stop working. As I have mentioned before, language is a very strong tool in the world of doing between people; but it becomes very difficult to use a tool of the world of doing to explain anything about the world of being. Anything that we can talk about or explain with words is already trapped between memory and time. Meditation is not based on memory, and it has nothing to do with time.

To understand what meditation is and how we can meditate, it is also important to understand what it is not, and I have found it quite useful to explain this to my patients and other truth seekers. Hopefully, based on what I clarify in this book, you too will get some clarity and be encouraged to find out for yourself first-hand.

Meditation is Not an Idea or Theory

Meditation is not a theory that was created, presented, or developed by anyone, and you can accept or reject it. Neither is it an idea of the divine self, as these are just ideas of one mask or a combination of masks. In the world of doing, masks have different ideas, and you learn them first from your parents or guardians, followed by teachers, peers, society, and your own experiences. Meditation cannot be an idea or theory because these are things you 'do' and, therefore, only exist in the world of doing.

Based on the example I gave you earlier, if you imagine that all of us were born in prison, everyone would produce some ideas about life within the walls of prison with the help of their five senses. They might also think about their experiences and what they have discovered, and present these discoveries to other people as philosophies, ideologies, and science, etc. Others could then compare these ideas to their own experiences and either accept or reject them and live accordingly.

Meditation is not another idea; it is not something that you 'do', and it cannot be done inside of the prison. It is not even a solution to any of the problems caused by living inside the prison.

Meditation isn't something that you come up with or create. Meditation can only be realised, and it can only be felt.

Even though you may have found some of the 'meditation techniques' useful and beneficial, that is because they are relaxation techniques.

Meditation is Not Relaxation

This is one of the most common misconceptions about meditation. There is much confusion about the meaning and definition of meditation; what people typically call meditation is mostly relaxation. In the world of doing, relaxation can be used to make life easier for the masks inside of a prison or on the stage, and it helps them to perform better. I am not against relaxation at all; on the contrary, I know that relaxation in any form is one of the most useful techniques in the world of doing. Anything directly or indirectly related to your doing, such as your memory, concentration, creativity, and every other aspect of your life, can be enhanced by relaxation, and you'll benefit hugely.

People are relaxed by different things, such as listening to music, dancing, singing, going on holiday, reading, writing, walking in nature, visiting friends, being with family, praying in a holy place, and simply closing their eyes and thinking about good things. But none of these pleasant methods are meditation.

Also, nowadays, these methods are not effective enough, and a lot of people need chemical help such as alcohol and drugs. Statistics show that in the UK, approximately 1 in 10 in men (8.7%) and 1 in 20 in women (3.3%) show signs of alcohol dependence known as alcoholism, and I am sure that the statistics on drug misuse in the UK are equally high.

Later in this chapter I will explain the two main categories of relaxation related to meditation.

Meditation is Not an Antidote for Depression, Stress or Anxiety

Over the years, I have heard many of my patients, friends, and other people say that meditation is good for treating or at least reducing depression, stress, and anxiety. When I asked them to give me examples, I realised that what they were talking about were different methods of relaxation. Obviously, when they signed up for a meditation course, that is what they expected and thought that was what they had done. I cannot go into common mental health conditions in this book in any great depth, but I will say that depression, stress, and anxiety do not exist. Again, I am not dismissing what anyone is experiencing, but what we are referring to as conditions are actually reactions of masks to both outside and inside stimulants in different ways. When these reactions cause disharmony, we begin to believe they exist and try to get rid of them. These common conditions (depression, stress, and anxiety) can be transformed into each other; in other words, one disharmony can cause the other one.

Let's suppose you (a man) fall in love with someone you know (a woman) and would like to start a relationship with her. You keep thinking about her, and you genuinely believe you are good enough to try and build up a relationship and invite her on a date. Your feelings get stronger until one day you decide to try your luck. When you're just about to contact her, some form of anxiety starts in your mind and pushes you out of your normal balance, and if it continues, this anxiety ends up affecting you physically and mentally.

However, one day you decide to ask her out at all costs. On that day, anxiety causes stress as you think about your outfit, what you are going to say, and finding the right time and place. Everything you think, plan, and want to do becomes stressful because you are not sure if you are going to get the outcome you want. In this example, your anxiety and stress come from the future and affect your present time. Then if she rejects you and you try again with no success, your anxiety will be replaced by depression.

My point is since anxiety is connected to the future and depression is connected to the past, and time is a 'concept' created by masks, all emotional distress is created by our masks as well, and they do not exist.

The same is true of darkness. You can define light because it exists, but when it comes to defining darkness, you still need to use light to explain that darkness is the absence of light. Why? Well, because you cannot define things that do not exist.

When your masks need to control results in the future, they cause anxiety in the present. If you cannot, your anxiety moves from the present to the past, and it becomes depression. The key is both anxiety and depression belong to the future and the past cannot exist, and if you keep your mind in the present moment, these mental disorders will disappear.

Coming back to my opening point, meditation has nothing to do with time — past or future, memory, or imagination — and therefore it cannot be an antidote for depression, anxiety, or stress. Relaxation, however, does calm the mind and encourages it to face reality and stay in the present moment, which is helpful for mental health.

Meditation is not about Improving your Concentration and Focus

I have come across several techniques of relaxation called 'meditation' that offer people improved concentration and focus. They ask you to concentrate on an object such as a flower or focus on a word or mantra – but as I said, these are forms of relaxation. The majority of people find it difficult at first, but after some practice they find a level of relaxation and improvement in their studies or work, and are able to focus on what they want or plan to do.

We all know that the basis of modern education is memory, skill, and the imagination to study – memorising theories from the past and designing new things by using our imagination.

The Cambridge dictionary definition of the word concentration is the ability to think carefully about something you are doing and nothing else.

Without concentration we would not be able to achieve any progress in our civilisation, but as meditation is not about doing anything and does not exist in the world of doing, it does not require concentration, and it does not improve it.

Meditation is Not Mindfulness

Unfortunately, people often connect meditation with mindfulness. The techniques to achieve mindfulness have nothing to do with meditation. Even though by now you might be thinking about how the techniques of achieving mindfulness fall into the category of being, I assure you, they do not.

In the Oxford dictionary, the definition of 'mindfulness' is described as a borrowed technique from Zen Buddhism and is defined as: "A mental state achieved by concentrating on the present moment, while calmly accepting the feelings and thoughts that come to you, used as a technique to help you relax."

By now, it should be clear that this is not meditation because it is a relaxation technique. Moreover, it is a method to obtain relaxation by making our minds full and accepting our feelings and thoughts. But who exactly is watching and accepting our thoughts? Our masks, of course! Since masks only exist in the world of doing, you can see why this is not meditation. However, you can and *should* use mindfulness techniques as a man or woman, husband or wife, teacher or student, and so on, as mindfulness is a very effective relaxation technique. It can help people avoid reaching anxious and depressed states in certain situations by training the mind to focus on the present moment.

Meditation is Not Contemplation

It is quite common to think that meditation is about sitting back and contemplating, because that idea is widely spread around the world. The Oxford dictionary explains the meaning of contemplation as: "The act of looking at something in a calm and careful way." This means that contemplation is the act of a mature, wise mind that has the ability to calmly and carefully analyse different things and find the points that other people usually miss. If we accept that our masks should be able to adapt to different situations and, at the same time, make progress, we need to admit that contemplation must be a very important part of our daily lives.

Contemplating frequently will help your masks become more observant, patient, and wise; these are the three most essential qualities for living happily in the world of doing. By now, you probably know why contemplation is not meditation. Who watches carefully and analyses your situation? Your masks! Since everything about contemplation is related to the world of doing, and meditation has nothing to do your masks or the world of doing, it cannot be contemplation.

Meditation is Not about Disabling the Brain and Mind

Since we have been discussing how meditation is not about doing anything, one might think it could mean disabling the brain and the mind – that is not the case either. This idea is just another cause of the confusion between relaxation and meditation.

Many people believe that, in order to meditate, one needs to reduce their mental activities, and as their mind is in their brain they have to stop or at least reduce their brain activities as well. Obviously, the mind is a combination of different masks and works mainly based on memory and imagination, and if you don't have any control over it, you won't be able to relax. Then again, this can be achieved through relaxation techniques.

The thing is, people try to boost and increase their brain activity by taking chemical stimulants such as caffeine in the morning and throughout the day, and then try to slow it down and relax by consuming alcohol in the evening. This has led them to believe that controlling the mind can happen only by pressurising the brain.

As I have explained before, and will do again later on, mental activities in the world of doing are based on masks and the private conversations you have between at least two of them in your mind. When it gets out of control, it causes so many symptoms of poor mental health such as depression and anxiety, and people believe that they can use meditation to reduce their brain activity in order to find some relaxation.

All of our organs, including the brain, are functioning to keep you alive and healthy. It has taken approximately 4.54 billion years for a piece of soil to become your brain, and now you want it to stop working? Of course, relaxation can help reduce the unnatural pressure against your mind; but again, relaxation has nothing to do with meditation. Meditation can happen to you only if all of your organs, including your brain, are in harmony with one another.

Meditation is Not about Teaching Techniques, Learning, or Practicing

The moment you hear about a meditation technique, you should know it is not meditation. The moment someone says that they can 'teach' you meditation, you should know it is *not* meditation. And the moment someone tells you to learn or practice meditation, you should know what they are talking about is not meditation. Why? Let's see.

In the world of doing, every mask of ours needs to learn new skills from teachers and others in order to improve its performance. Moreover, one has to practice in order to get better and better, like playing the piano.

As meditation has nothing to do with the world of doing, there is nothing to learn or practice in order to do it better. When you see adverts or posts for learning meditation, it is actually about learning different forms of relaxation — which I recommend you try — but, from my point of view, is not meditation.

Going back to my example of life in prison, inside you can learn everything from cooking to exercising to culture to the law, which will help make life easier for yourself and others. But as meditation is about life outside the prison, it doesn't teach you anything and there is nothing to learn. You cannot teach or learn your realisation of life! It has to come from within.

Meditation is Not a Journey of Self-discovery

We have been told by our level 1 mask providers such as parents, teachers, and religious leaders that self-improvement is a great virtue, and sooner or later we'll need to pay attention to it. That is why many people try to find and experiment with different tools to that end.

Some books and courses lead people to believe that meditation is a journey of self-discovery. They think that meditation is like a journey — beginning at a starting point and moving towards finding yourself as a destination — but the reality is quite different.

Self-discovery involves masks; only masks experience a process of discovering and move forward to achieve new skills, a better quality of life, and even relaxation. Relaxation can help you look at your masks, identify them, and use them smartly, but this has nothing to do with meditation.

Meditation is not a movement. It does not involve an experience of you reaching somewhere, so there is no starting point or destination. When there is ultimate stillness, and you have no movement whatsoever, you might experience meditation. Therefore, it cannot be a journey.

Meditation is Not about Seeking Happiness and Calmness

Some of my patients and friends have told me over the years that whenever they were meditating, they felt happier and calmer. If you are seeking happiness and calmness, you might enjoy relaxation, exercising, and learning new skills – but happiness and calmness are not something you find. They are the result of your harmony inside and outside with the whole world of doing.

It is very natural for your masks to be interested in happiness and calmness as these states of mind help masks function better, but you can create these pleasant feelings with relaxation and, of course, by achieving your goals. Children are generally happy unless someone makes them unhappy because their happiness is typically based on their being, and adults are mostly unhappy unless someone makes them happy because their happiness is based on their doing. I will go into this theory in more detail in the next chapter.

The point is, if you're 'finding' something, you are doing something, and only masks in the world of doing can seek something. Meditation has nothing to do with seeking happiness and calmness; it is about realisation.

Meditation is Not about Improving your Health

The Cambridge dictionary definition of the word health is: "The condition of the body and the degree to which it is free from illness, or the state of being well."

From a holistic point of view, health is not the absence of disease, and it is not a level or stage of your life when you are pain- and disease-free, as these are natural parts of life. Health is the natural attitude towards whatever happens in life (including disease) in order to find harmony inside and outside. You can be free from pain and disease with a very ill attitude towards life and, sooner or later, this will catch up with your body and mind (or both), and you will become ill and suffer. Similarly, you can be ill with a healthy attitude and very soon, your system will become as healthy as possible.

In a traditional, holistic approach to life, illness doesn't exist. Health is harmony, and disease is an imaginary form of disharmony. Let's say that health has a thousand levels. Below 500, you start to feel ill. Below 400, you definitely feel ill and begin to seek help. Below 300 you see your doctor, below 200 you need serious treatment, and below 100 your doctors cannot do anything for you. But if your health is at level 501, doctors are not interested in your health anymore. Yet there is a huge difference between 501 and 1000. Regardless of whatever level you're at, you are healthier than the levels below and less healthy than the levels above. It is not a black and white picture, and you cannot be ill or healthy. You can be *healthier* or *less healthy* depending on the attitude you have towards life. At any level you can try to become healthier, and relaxation is a great way to achieve this.

As most of the physical and mental problems relate to your masks, finding solutions needs to be done by studying them. As we have said before, meditation does not happen when you are using masks because masks belong to the world of doing; therefore, it is 'relaxation' that can show you the right ways of improving your health.

Meditation, Happiness, and Well-being

Everything people do is to obtain, maintain, and increase their happiness and well-being: living in a society, having a family, maintaining relationships, pursuing education, following religions, improving medicine and technology, and engineering in all its forms. Even wars are fought for peace according to some political leaders. My point is, in the world of doing all the doings are focused on finding happiness and well-being.

People need a guarantee for everything they or others do. For example, imagine you have been offered two phones. Both of them have good features, but only one comes with a guarantee. Which one would you choose? Obviously, the one with a guarantee. Similarly, in the world of emotions, promises are like guarantees. If you start your family with someone who loves you, you have a better guarantee of staying together and bringing up your children in a family unit as opposed to getting married to someone where there is no love, on a contract basis only.

Human beings have developed different ways of securing these guarantees, such as creating tools, routines, and habits. But the fact that there are so many progressive mental and emotional diseases in our current world proves that masks cannot achieve the depth of happiness they desire, and if they find it superficially, they are not able to maintain it.

In other words, masks in the world of doing might achieve some level of well-being or happiness, but it is not reliable, and they will need to increase the level of 'guarantee' with top-ups in the form of psychological and chemical help.

Based on what I have explained, I hope that it is clear how valuable relaxation can be in increasing your chance of getting more guarantees from your actions and reactions.

Later on, I will also explain how meditation destroys all guarantees because they belong to the world of being. In prison, there are accurate guarantees for most aspects of your life. You know, for example, what you can have for lunch on any particular day, week, month, or year. But when you get out of the prison, there is no guarantee of what you will eat, wear, or even where you'll sleep. Meditation cannot be used to give guarantees for a better life, or more happiness and well-being. Meditation does not promise, offer, or improve anything.

What is Meditation?

After explaining what meditation is not, we can now discuss what meditation *is*, and I will be explaining this through language we use in the world of doing.

Meditation is a kind of realisation and awareness of the unlimited world of being. As shown in diagram 1 (Chapter 3), the world of being is like a circle of infinite circumference with a very limited concentric circle inside itself called the world of doing. Using the example I gave you at the beginning of this chapter, if the world of doing is like a prison, meditation is realising you also exist outside of the prison, and therefore all of your tools and guarantees automatically become unusable.

Meditation as inner wisdom or enlightenment is not about doing anything; in fact, it can only happen when you stop doing everything. Meditation is some kind of realisation – a state of consciousness and awareness of your existence and your growth potential in the world of being.

Masks need protection, and that is the reason why they are very defensive. Tools like relaxation can help your masks to protect themselves and improve their quality of life, but meditation is about becoming aware of the whole of your existence and your growth inside the amazing network of life.

One might consider that removing one's blockages and getting rid of the obstacles to growth are the main results of meditation, but that is not something that you learn, teach, practice, or expect as a result. For example, babies do not want to be separated from their mothers, and that is why they cry if that happens. As they grow, they are able to stay with others as long as their mothers are around until they eventually go to school and finally become an adult and live independently in a separate place. These changes are not something you teach them – it happens as they grow up.

If this growing process carries on, people should be ready to leave their body behind and move on to the next stage of their lives. But if the growing process stops then there is fear, and people stop moving forward, and death becomes the root of all the negatives in their lives.

If the masks you use in the world of doing are not suitable for you, or you don't know how to manage them, they will slow down or even stop you from growing. This resistance causes pain and suffering because everything else grows and keeps moving. Therefore, by using all of the tools available to you such as deep relaxation, you can prepare yourself to experience meditation which will help you unblock your blockages and enable you to carry on growing.

As you know, growing is about nourishing inside and outside in a way that nature wants. For a child to grow, you need to provide food, water, shelter, and education, but this has to be done naturally. You would not force-feed a child and expect them to grow better and faster. They need to be able to digest what they eat at their own speed. They also don't need to know about human anatomy and physiology in order to grow.

In the same way, you cannot force meditation, but you can nourish and prepare yourself for it by using relaxation methods in a particular way. If you see someone sitting under a tree with their eyes closed, it is not necessarily because they are meditating. What you see is just preparation for meditation. Relaxation only in one form can help you become ready for meditation to happen. Meditation is a realisation and direct awareness of your life in the world of being with no mediator (mask) to feel or comment on the truth. Applying some of the following relaxation types can help that realisation occur.

Relaxation Types

Relaxation, as one of the essential tools in the world of doing, can be used in two totally different ways: relaxation based on obtaining guarantees, and relaxation based on losing guarantees.

Relaxation based on Obtaining Guarantees

As explained, life in the world of doing is mainly based on obtaining guarantees for finding, maintaining, and increasing happiness and well-being. It is evident that if you are relaxed, you will get more guarantees of better results in whatever you do. Studies have shown that having a relaxed state of mind improves concentration and helps performance in exams. While a stressed state of mind, regardless of how much it has studied, will not perform to its full capability. That in itself proves the importance of relaxation for gaining a higher level of happiness and well-being in the world doing.

Relaxation based on Losing Guarantees

The second and more critical type of relaxation is the one that can help you prepare for meditation to happen. As meditation happens to you when you are ready to become aware of your life in the world of being, and feeling your life and existence out of prison, this type of relaxation will help you lose your guarantees. For example, sitting somewhere nice and quiet in a pleasant environment, not hot and not cold, with no noise pollution and no disturbances, will make you relaxed and increase the chances of your awareness moving outside of the walls of safety or your prison.

You make a wall of safety and guarantee out of your money, another wall out of your relationship, another one out of your personal philosophy or religion, and another out of your gender. There could be many other walls made from every important thing in your life as long as they give you more guarantees for finding more happiness and well-being.

However, one day that living space will become your torment as, between these walls that you have been making thicker and thicker, you will realise that you forgot to build any doors in them. Any safe place, even a palace that does not give you the choice and freedom to move in and out, becomes a prison. Once you realise you are trapped, you will try to free yourself. This urge to break free is what Lao Tzu, Buddha, and all the other respectful, spiritual leaders have mentioned. The question that still remains is how?

Every single philosophy, ideology, and method such as Taoism, Buddhism, Hinduism, and Zen have their strategies and solutions for creating space for meditation to happen. But again, the problem for people of the 21st century is that they do not possess enough time to spend a massive part of their lives in temples, following gurus and masters. These old methods naturally have no guarantee and are too complicated to follow.

As I have mentioned before, I do not claim that I have the right tools for you to free yourself from the prison that you have unintentionally created. But I am willing to share with you what I have found over the years as an effortless, practical, and efficient way of using the second type of relaxation. This, again, is not *the* way; it is *a* way to prepare yourself for meditation and subsequent enlightenment.

Before I start to explain in the chapters that follow what I found, I would like to mention some important points that will help you achieve the results you want:

a. I do not have a time limit for using any tools, and it will be different for everyone – from a few seconds to years. So, the question of how long you think it will take for you to use these tools and get results is nonsense. There is no time limit for using tools and getting results.

b. These tools are my first selection as the easiest to understand and follow. They are the most efficient, practical, and up-to-date for the 21st century, and are relevant for the preparation of mediation, based on my personal experience and observation.

c. These tools can be used by anyone regardless of their age, gender, nationality, or religion, and they do not require any previous experience or knowledge of eastern philosophy, using equipment, learning a new language, converting your belief system, or giving up any of your masks. Using these tools will make your life easier and provide an excellent platform for meditation to happen.

d. These tools were discovered and designed by many masters over the years to help you go inside of the core of your existence, so please don't evaluate them in the same way as assessing the tools you use for the outside world.

e. As you know, there is no guarantee that meditation or

enlightenment will happen even when you use all these tools correctly. Meditation will happen to your 'self', not your 'I', when you become quiet and stop doing everything and allow the muddy water of your mind to become clear by leaving it alone. Expecting results is not leaving your mind alone, and meditation will almost certainly not happen when your mind is busy with expectations.

f. Even though these tools require no one but yourself, as they are for self-relaxation, it is okay to reach out to someone you believe might guide you better.

g. If you suffer from any psychological or emotional diseases or disorders, please consult your doctor before you use any of these tools. These tools are just a recommendation for relaxation and not a substitute for any mental and psychological treatments.

h. After trying the tools I suggest in this book, I would like you to use your creativity to find or design new tools for yourself and experiment with them to choose the ones that work best for you.

9

PAST, PRESENT, AND FUTURE

As I've established, in the world of doing we need masks to be able to perform, and masks need memory and imagination to function. Memory and imagination need a timeline in our lives to put all of the events on and to help masks function. Time in our mind gets divided into three sections: the past, present, and future, but neither memory nor imagination can work in the present time. We have created the illusion of time with a huge amount of past, a smaller part of future and a very tiny bridge between those two as present.

Now, everything that you have understood, studied, earned, experienced, done, accepted, rejected, and remembered, etc. comes from your memory by pretending that the past exists. Anything that you want to do — all your plans, expectations, and anticipation — comes from the future by using your imagination which still is mainly based on your memory and the past. So the main question is, if your mind uses your memory to connect to the past and your imagination to connect to the future on the timeline of the world of doing, what tool do you have to connect to the present time?

Since the past and the future do not exist, your body cannot live in either of them and cannot use any air, food, or water from the past or the future. Yet your mind lives mainly in the past and the future and has no tools to connect to your life in the present moment. This conflict is the root of so many physical and psychological diseases and disorders. Your body is constantly dealing with many functions, actions, and reactions by using hormones. When your mind is using a negative or depressing memory from the past (which in reality doesn't exist), it affects your hormones, and consequently imbalances them which can cause both physical and mental problems.

The masks you have accepted from your parents, friends, society, teachers, etc. have taught you every essential thing from the past in order for you to live a better future. In this way, you have more guarantees and a better chance of gaining the results you want. That is why when you want to say something is useless and unworkable, you say that it has no future. If the level of guarantee goes down (due to an unsuitable past that can affect the future), people feel depressed and anxious as they don't have any control over what will happen next.

That said, there are occasions in your masks' experiences, such as listening to a live orchestra, that if you are busy appreciating the past (and thinking how beautiful the music is compared to what you have heard before) or concerned about the future (by thinking about what they are going to play next), you will miss the enjoyment of listening in an expanded present moment.

But the question remains, if the past and the future do not exist, why is your mind under the impression that it can live in the past or future? The reason is that we have created a reporter in our mind to talk to our masks about the past and the future. When you are silent, but there is a private conversation going on in your mind, and that conversation is between at least one of your masks and the reporter.

The mind cannot be one as it needs that inner conversation to make the past and future feel real.

My main question to you then is, do you want to live and feel your life, or do you want to be a reporter and report everything that is passing or has already passed and is going to pass you by?

It is the same as a football reporter – they don't play, but they keep reporting on what just has happened. Even when you try to meditate, the reporter tries to make a report out of it and directs your attention to how effective it should be and the tools of relaxation and so on.

Based on what most people learn from others, they believe that their presence is the result of the past, and if you want to understand anything in your present time, you have to go back to the past and study its history. Whereas, the past doesn't exist, and so it cannot cause anything to happen. Life has to happen in this very present moment, in all dimensions and directions – it is not linear. Our memories create the past by remembering what is happening now and creating a timeline. The knowledge of humankind has been passed on through time using language, and the character of language is linear. One word at a time forms a line, a paragraph, a page, and so on. Everything that you know is understood in a line and enables you to talk about life and teach different aspects of it from the past, but you won't be able to feel it, as life is happening in all dimensions and directions right now and at the same time.

So, the past and the future are illusions, and they have nothing to do with real life. Remembering what happened in the past is a very useful way of creating tools and improving skills, but the present is not the result of it. It's the same as travelling by boat from point A to B. The wake at the back of the boat can show you the movement and the direction the boat is going, but it has no power to change or control the movement, direction, or speed of it. The past is a recording method for what has happened, but it is not the reality. Just as a food menu is a record of food, but it is not the food you can eat.

As I promised at the beginning, I will not discuss any ideas that are not practically useful to you. So the question is: how does the fact that your past is the result of your present help you in your daily life and ultimately help you prepare for meditation to happen and experience awakening?

Reviewing the past is very useful if you can learn from your experience and avoid making the same mistakes in the present. But the problem is, if you cannot see your situation in the present moment, you have to wait for your present to become your past, and then analyse it and learn from it. For example, you trusted someone enough to do business with them yesterday, and then you discovered later that the person betrayed you and took your money. Now today you regret it and think you know that person, but it's too late. My point is that yesterday you were not capable of knowing that stranger, and it was a deficiency in the present time. Now today you may know that person, but you still suffer from wisdom deficiency because you don't have a connection with your present time.

The fact that your past is the result of your present will enable you to do something about your wisdom or knowledge deficiency today. By tomorrow, your today will become your past, and you won't be able to do anything about it.

Most people feel pressure about the past because they believe they should have done something and missed their opportunity, or they shouldn't have done something but they did. As you can see, guilt comes from the past based on your judgments against yourself. To save energy and avoid the guilt of making mistakes, people try to learn from the past and discover patterns to create new habits. Then over time, they realise that those habits are not always helpful and put them in two categories of good, like exercising, and bad, like smoking. Breaking habits is very difficult and sometimes impossible for your masks as they are part of your mask's package. The patterns and stereotypes of masks such as jobs, gender, age, etc. are based on observation of the past.

So the past is the result of the present! Whatever your masks do will be your past soon, so by paying attention to your present moment you can change your past. But the reporter in your mind takes you to either the past with lots of regret and eventually depression, or to the future which causes lots of anxiety and fear.

The second form of relaxation (losing guarantees) that I mentioned in the previous chapter only works with the present moment neither by denying what has happened in the past nor anticipating the future, but by accepting life as it comes to the present moment and then disappearing. Understanding the concept of the present time and becoming relaxed by disconnecting your mind from the past or the future will help you to get rid of the reporter in your mind, and you can become silent and one! That is precisely what you need to prepare yourself for meditation to happen.

Relaxation with no guarantee helps you connect with the present moment and accept the natural course of events as they come and go – exactly the same as dancing to music, not fast with a rush and not slow causing resistance. When you feel relaxed and allow the illusion of the past and the future to disappear, meditation might happen to you, and you will feel the world of being and that we are all living in an eternal now.

10

INNER WORK

The focus of this chapter is to discuss what kind of inner work you need to do to prepare yourself for hosting meditation.

For some people, the inner world is their spiritual connection, and for others, it is related to their mental or emotional field. However, for all the masks in the world of doing, regardless of their different belief systems, personal philosophies, religions, nationalities, backgrounds, genders, and social levels, the inner world refers to the private conversation between at least one of these masks and the reporter in their mind. In other words, the meaning of 'I' or 'my mind', 'inside of my mind', 'me', and 'my personal space', refers to this inner world.

Almost everyone in your life wants to teach you something about the outside world; how to look at it, how to analyse it, and what to do about it. If you obey your mask providers and do what they ask you to do, you will be a good mask such as a good son, an ideal husband or wife, a good citizen, etc. Otherwise, you will be punished in different ways, from simple criticisms to mask providers cancelling their contract with you and returning their mask if possible. Therefore, in the world of doing, you have learnt what to do related to the outside world to make life easier for yourself. In other words, what to do to create more happiness and well-being.

Working with the outer world is not that easy, and you learn some kind of engineering over the years to create and make what you need if it does not exist, and modify what is already available, in order to become more useful. Engineering is not only helpful in building machines but also in building relationships, a kind of psychological engineering. You read books, learn from experts, experiment, and use your mistakes as ways of learning how to make your outside world more pleasant and closest to what you expect. Without getting help from these systems that teach you what and how to do it, it is almost impossible to carry on living successfully in the world of doing.

Yet when it comes to your inner world, you are on your own. You hear something from your parents, teachers, friends, or others about inner happiness and well-being. Still, the level of information you have compared to what you need is like trying to assemble an aeroplane without having any engineering experience or instructions, and then using your mistakes purely from the past! Obviously, the result won't be good, which is why we are seeing mental and emotional diseases and disorders increasing at a rapid rate.

At school, you learn almost everything about the outside world in different subjects, but there are no lessons on what to do with yourself. Even religion and spiritual philosophies are taught as history, and the rest is just an invitation from your level 1 masks to believe in what they say even though they are not entirely convinced themselves. Obviously, if you are not sure about something, you have only two ways of dealing with it – you either believe or disbelieve, and the latter has consequences and potentially unpleasant reactions from your mask providers.

Thanks largely to technology, the 21st century is the century of information. In the past, you needed to spend a lot of time in libraries or visiting subject matter experts and specialists to conduct research, but now everyone has access to information at the touch of a smartphone. But what are you going to do with the information you get for your inner world? It is like receiving a list of ingredients. How you are going to cook with them?

Imagine you order a very good car and all the parts are delivered to your home in different boxes. You look at the boxes and complain that this isn't a car, but you're told that all the parts are there and it is up to you how to put them together. You cannot leave the boxes outside, so you take them in and store them all over your house. It would be so difficult and frustrating. On one hand, you still need a car, and all you have are car parts; and on the other hand, your living space is totally taken over by all of these boxes. So, in the same manner, people get information about the inner world, meditation, relaxation, self-esteem, self-love, happiness, well-being, etc. but they don't have any engineering skills or knowledge to assemble and make them useful.

For inner work, the second type of relaxation can help. First, you need to get rid of all of the influences and expectations of your masks, especially from level 1. That is the first step in your journey to freedom. Then you can do your research about the many different systems of building your inner engineering skills such as Taoism, Buddhism, Zen and psychology. I am not trying to recommend any one system to you as you must find it for yourself once you are free from all of the influences and biased ideas that have come from your mask providers. When you are relaxed, reading books, learning from teachers and masters, contemplating different aspects of life and making inner observations, some other instrumental techniques will become very useful to you. I will explain how some of them can be helpful to you in building up your connection to your inner intelligence and wisdom.

11

NO BONDING

In the world of doing, masks feel that they are always under attack, which is why fear is one of the strongest emotions people experience in their lives – from straightforward fears of heights and saying 'no' to level 1 mask providers to very complex kinds of fear of not achieving goals and failure. This emotion causes some of the biggest problems in people's lives.

There are many sources of fear for the masks in your life, but I am going to concentrate on some of the main ones I have seen in my own life and that I have observed in others.

a. The number one source of fear in the world of doing is the idea of death. When you pay attention to people's fear and reactions towards death, you realise it's the *idea* that people are afraid of, not death itself. Why? Because death would be the end of the world of doing and the existence of all masks. That is the reason why when people think about death, they think about their mask providers such as parents, children, spouse, wealth, name, reputation, and plans for the future. All of these are related to masks and masks are afraid of disappearing. For the same reason, masks resist against real meditation because that makes them disappear.

You should know that you experience a mini death every night when you go to sleep. Are you afraid of sleeping? Does it matter if you sleep for five hours or five million years? Isn't it true that when you go to sleep, the whole world, including your masks and their providers and what you scientifically know about the world, disappears? So what are you afraid of? Practically speaking, it is not the act of going to sleep – it is thinking about what happens if you don't wake up. You put this thought into your timeline, and it causes fear because it means that you will go to sleep forever.

So the only way people have dealt with this thought (which is the primary source of fear) is by keeping themselves busy with normal every daily life: relationships, working, eating, and drinking. All of the mask's activities can be used for distracting your mind from thinking about death. The other way is bonding: bonding with mask providers by going on holiday, or to parties with friends, or another is by creating God in your mind and bonding with the idea of divine.

b. Mask provider's standards. Every mask provider has some rules and requirements. If you are a bad mask, they might ask you to return their mask, or if it is not possible, they might give you a negative title. For example, your parents may have some expectations of you, and if you want to be a good son or daughter, you need to understand what they expect and do what they want at the right time. If they change their standards or if you are not able to do everything that they want, you will feel fear.

Another example is your employer's standards. If you are not good enough in the way that your boss wants, you might get penalised or even lose your job (and your mask). That is why when you accept a mask from a provider – you need to continually analyse their standards and your abilities and timing in the overall situation, and this can cause fear.

Bonding with your mask provider gives you more guarantees of keeping your mask and reduces your fear. If you are your parents' favourite child, you will get the title of a good son or daughter much easier. Likewise, if you bond with your boss, the chances of keeping your job and getting promoted increases, and the fear of losing your job decreases.

If you want to feel your life behind your masks and prepare yourself for meditation, you need to free your mind from the importance of your masks and stop bonding with your mask providers. Please note that I am not suggesting that you disconnect from your mask providers entirely.

c. As I have explained before, both time and memory are created by your masks for you to be able to function in the world of doing. But the concept of time can cause fear in both the short and long term. In the short term, your masks have minimal time to finish specific tasks and achieve desirable results. In the long term, some of the more appealing aspects of your masks are getting weaker over time, and you call it the age affect. You are afraid of losing your beauty, power, sexual energy, memory, concentration, and intelligence, to name a few.

That is why you bond with some masks and even some memories of your childhood or adolescence and don't want to let that time go. Cosmetic surgery, fashion, and language are just some of the ways you can bond with your memories against the effects of time.

d. Accepting new masks can also cause fear. Why? Because on one hand you think the new masks can bring certain benefits, but on the other hand finding the right level for them, and the possibility of the new mask becoming negative, causes fear and some anxiety for you. You might need to justify your new mask to the related masks. For example, if you have a new colleague and you need to go for a dinner meeting, you may need to justify it to your husband or wife. That can potentially cause fear of being misjudged. In the world of doing, everything that you do relates to at least one mask, if not more. Justifying and finding the right purpose for what you do concerning the masks you have accepted can cause fear.

e. Competition, criticism and attacks from other masks can cause a huge amount of fear. If you are applying for your dream job, you need to compete with all of the other applicants, and that causes fear. Also, to avoid criticism from your current mask providers, you need to justify everything that you do, and that can create fear and stress as well. That is why people have created words like 'intent' and 'purpose' to explain the reason behind their decisions and find justification for what they do.

Intent means you have a plan in mind for something that you have decided to do either soon or sometime in the future. The question is how this relates to your masks and how beneficial it would be for you and your masks provider. This process can potentially cause some fear. For example, imagine you want to use your family savings to start a business. You need to justify your actions to the other mask providers such as your husband or wife, your parents, and your children. That is why people have created expressions like 'mean to do something', 'looking to do something' and 'going to do something' to bond with their mask providers and reduce their fear. In severe situations, people use words like 'purpose' in different forms such as aims, goals, and objectives to reduce their fear and create a safe platform on which to bond with their mask providers.

In the world of doing, for most things that you do and would like to explain to others, you will need to relate to your masks and sometimes even to a mask that you have provided for yourself. This is because your actions and reactions need to be part of a network to be justified. The network could be as small as your personal and family network or as big as your social and global network.

f. Natural disasters, accidents, and incidents outside your control also cause fear. You might have an accident and damage your body badly, or you lose your job due to the financial crisis in the market. These situations can affect you and your life in the world of doing. Regardless of whether it is your fault or not, still, the situation can cause a huge amount of fear and stress for you and your mask providers.

I am sure that you can find many other sources for your fear by observing and contemplating your daily life, but for all of the reasons above, people have learned to bond with others. They believe that their fear will be reduced if they bond with their mask providers (especially in levels 1 and 2) and even their own masks. For example, they may change their accent around friends or colleagues, or they may change their hair colour or skin colour to suit another. So bonding with others from a low to a high level is based on fear and pleasing mask providers.

However, in order to prepare yourself for meditation, you need to stop bonding with anyone and anything, and not take sides under any circumstances. If you would like to feel yourself behind your masks and meditate, you need to let your masks melt down and disappear, at least temporarily. If you are bonding with other masks or mask providers, you won't be able to meditate. That is the reason why people in the public eye, specifically, struggle to let their masks to disappear. These people have millions of mask providers in the form of fans. The more people you have attached to you, the harder it is to move, the narrower the passage of life becomes, and the more energy required to live your life.

12

DETOXIFYING BODY AND MIND

In the world of doing, our existence is on a spectrum ranging from the physical, mental, and emotional to the spiritual. Anything that happens to any side of the spectrum, be it positive or negative, can affect the other side, and that is why it is so important to look after the entire spectrum holistically.

I am not going to explain the benefits of a clean diet, hydration, exercise, and breathing correctly as you can research the physical side of detoxification and experiment with well-known methods. In this chapter, I would like to highlight how masks can produce poison in both your mind and your body.

If one of your masks produces a negative emotion such as anger, sadness, or anxiety, that emotion can affect your hormonal balance and may cause pressure on your nervous system. By looking after your masks and understanding the way that they work, you can not only prevent your body and mind from being poisoned by toxins, but you can also detoxify them from the toxins from the past.

Masks need to be strengthened or upgraded by mask providers. In the case of a woman with the mask of a wife, the provider is her husband and she needs his attention and confirmation of his love to find her mask safe. This is the main reason that the masks in level 1 and level 2 are responsible for so many mental and emotional diseases and disorders. Why? Because as I have explained, if something goes wrong with one of your mask providers in a lower level, you can get help from a mask provider in the highest level. But if something happens to your relationship with a mask provider in the highest level, then you have no choice but to get help from a provider in a lower level, and that causes poison. For example, if you had a problem with your business partner, when you got home you could talk to your husband or wife for comfort as well as advice. But if you have a problem with your spouse and you talk to your business partner, you would cause poison in your system.

In over 40 years of working with people and patients professionally, I have never seen a case of mental and emotional disease or disorder that was not caused by their level 1 or 2 mask providers, except for those cases where there is a genetic, congenital, or physiological deficiency or defect. That is why, when I see a patient with a physiological problem, I pay attention to their stress level and emotional and mental pressure in relation to their level 1 and level 2 mask providers. All of the psychosomatic cases are excellent and clear examples of this rule.

In my opinion, one of the most important and common causes of poison in the mind and of course in the body is 'neediness'. The poison that is produced by neediness works like a lamination over both good and bad emotions in a way you don't see or feel. Neediness can act as a layer around love, care, sympathy, empathy, fear, hope, anger, stress, anxiety, disappointment, loneliness, and excitement in ways that you don't see. In the world of doing, the more you need something, the more likely you are to push it away and lose it, even with objects like your car, for example. The more you need it, the more likely it is to get a problem and not start - let alone people! When you need someone so much, you create poison which pushes them away from you. People find neediness as synonymous with love and care, and you often hear them say, "I love you and I need you" so it must be real love. But very soon they realise that they cannot live with that person anymore because the poison starts to affect them.

People need their masks to be able to perform in the world of doing, and masks always need their providers to top up their identity. This neediness produces poison and toxins that, in the long run, affect both your mind and body. When some couples want to show to each other and others that they have real love in their hearts, they call each other their 'other half'. So, to be complete, they need each other, and after a while that produces poison which affects them, and they separate and need to find *another* half.

You can accept masks and get rid of neediness in any form and still love your mask providers without needing them. As a complete person, you can love another complete person and celebrate life together rather than completing each other. You need to know that slowly, and over many years, masks can get used to some of the poisons and pain that affects them, but this process brings your mental and physical performance down to such a level that meditation will never happen to you. It is therefore so essential to detoxify your mind and emotions from all of the poisons and toxins produced by neediness, and of course, detoxify your physical body from all other sources of poison that come with a poor lifestyle.

13

CONNECTION BETWEEN DIFFERENT ASPECTS OF LIFE

In the world of being, existence is an infinite network, and everything is connected via being itself. As the world of doing is a tiny and finite circle inside the world of being, the same rule applies to it and everything is connected in both forms of being and doing.

Those who pay attention to this fact, and whose doing is based on connection, will not only find true happiness and fulfilment but also success in any goal they choose in the world of doing. Those who lose this connection in their mind and between different aspects of their lives will feel fear, stress, and anxiety. In other words, they feel disoriented and need to ask mask providers such as their parents, spouse, friends and in some cases, psychology experts and spiritual or religious leaders where they are and what they need to do next.

If you pay attention to your body, you will realise that everything, including all of your systems, organs, tissues, and cells, are connected. They also are connected to the outside world in terms of breathing, eating, drinking, seeing, hearing, smelling, tasting, and touching. They work together in a vast network, and any disharmony will cause disease, disorder, pain, and discomfort.

But what about your mind? Is it related to different aspects of your life such as your personal life, professional life, and social life? Masks are weak in terms of connection. If you want different aspects of your life and your performance on the stage of the world of doing to be connected harmoniously, you need to give them a lot of help.

But how do we know if different aspects of our lives are connected or not? The answer is easy. If something changes for one of your masks, let's say your relationship, does that change any other aspect of your life? For instance, if you were getting married or in the middle of a divorce, would that make any difference to your diet, exercise, or work? If not, that means there is no connection between the different aspects of your life.

Realising your connection in both the world of being and the world of doing is important and creates harmony with everything in your life. Why do people go to see a live orchestra? To listen to all of the different musicians individually or to listen to the amazing harmony they produce together, and the feeling it creates? If meditation doesn't happen in your life and you don't feel your existence behind your masks, what you have is a group of musicians playing for themselves with no conductor.

Obviously, we use our five senses to scan and analyse the outside world, but we do not process the feeling of life behind our masks because we are too busy identifying ourselves with our masks, and not feeling life in an unlimited world of being.

What happens to a ship or an aeroplane in the event they lose their radar connection? They have to count on verbal communication via radio to ask others at the control centre where they are and which direction to go in. Clearly, inventing language was a quick and effective channel of communication between the masks to understand one another (and I am using it now to communicate with you), but it has never been a good substitute for connection.

Your lack of connection to your digestive system has resulted in you needing to ask a nutritionist what to eat. In the same way, your lack of connection to your mind and the inner world has resulted in you needing to ask a psychologist or a counsellor how to control your thoughts and emotions. Another example is connection in relationships. When people fall in love or see each other, they usually express their love in a few words, but when they are separating, they need to use a lot of words to justify what they mean.

Nowadays, communication tools are so advanced and readily available that a couple living in the same house can send each other text messages while they are both in the same room. Emotions that could have been conveyed in facial expressions have been replaced by emojis, and family gatherings are being replaced by family WhatsApp groups. The less *connection* you have, the more *communication* you need.

Intellect is only one form of intelligence, and it is based on gathering data and information (either verbally or in written form) in order to zoom in and find more detail about any particular thing, situation, or subject. A human being is very well equipped to use many different forms of intelligence in their daily life, in the world of doing in both directions – zooming in to get more details and zooming out to see the bigger picture of life and have a better connection. Still, as society shows, people are moving towards a minimum connection with nature and each other and relying hugely on communication methods which consequently results in a loss of connection with the bigger picture.

This is the way that education, logic, and ideas work today in the world of doing. Compare children 100 years ago to now. Which children are connected to nature and the people around them? Ask some of the children around you today about the seasons and the changes in nature, and they are more likely to be more inclined to google it than look outside the window.

Our so-called knowledge is based on the contrast between the background and the objects themselves. Even the way we know ourselves is based on the background of our family, society, religion, and even the football club you support. Can you explain yourself without referencing someone or something else? I am a man as opposed to woman, hard-working as opposed to lazy, this nationality as opposed to another nationality, and so on.

Communication is a form of connection, but not all forms of connection can be explained as communication. Language, art, and music are different all forms of communication, but the connection is much broader and deeper than communication. For example, a couple can talk to each other but are not necessarily connected. Connection is a deep feeling like belonging to an unlimited and infinite network that is alive. Connection activates different software programmes in your mind that are in harmony with your body, which gives you access to different wisdom. That kind of knowledge cannot be obtained from the outside or learned from a teacher. Otherwise, we would have so many Beethovens graduating from music colleges every year.

Connection, in a comprehensive way. happens when you connect with your existence behind your masks. Without it, you will communicate with your masks or other people's masks for the rest of your life and become increasingly confused and unwell. When you close your eyes, you stop communicating to enhance your connection, and that can be an excellent foundation for meditation.

Connection gives you an exceptional feeling of finding your true nature behind your masks, which doesn't need justification. But all kinds of communication need to be justified, such as talking, writing, and teaching. The more you are connected to the core of existence, the happier, calmer, and wiser you will feel, and the less worried you will be about becoming or not becoming the mask you want.

14

YOUR CAPACITY TO PRODUCE LOVE

Love has been felt and described in so many ways, across all cultures and times. We have seen descriptions of love ranging from 'love is divine' to 'love is a feeling of physical temptation.' Well, it merely depends on the person's social and personal experience. In ancient Greek philosophy, you find different types of love from Agape (unconditional love) and Eros (romantic love) to Ludus (playful love) and Mania (obsessive love).

The world of doing is always happening; something or the other is always in motion. People are always getting rid of their lower-level masks and finding new ones, or they feel the need to promote masks to a higher level. Love is very often the common reason for these changes and promotions. Popular masks relate to love, and people experience it for the first time in childhood from their parents and later on with their siblings and friends. When they grow up, they learn to go to the marketplace to feed their emotional needs and find a lover to give them a mask of being loved. Clearly, when you go to get something from the market, you have to pay for it with whatever you can afford. The currency in this marketplace is beauty, age, wealth, health, fame, title, personality, and/or anything else that fits society's definition of a complete package.

In this chapter, I would like to offer you a new point of view on love – firstly, by giving you smart questions which you can use to examine your own love and that of your mask providers, and secondly, by showing you love's connection to meditation. I will start by explaining love in two different categories: 'common love' and 'real love', as related to masks in the world of doing. I will also explain some of the main characteristics of both based on my own contemplation and observation, and I am sure you can find many more for yourself.

Common Love

In my opinion, what people know as love and describe in different ways is only one type of neediness which has been used by people's various different masks. Your 'I' as ego and the common part of all your masks can feel neediness as different forms of love. When it comes to your children, for example, it could become unconditional love, and when it is towards your spouse, it could develop into romantic or obsessive love.

One of the first characteristics of common love is the existence of 'I' as the witness, reporter, and producer. When you love someone or something, that means you are the centre of the world, and you have found someone or something very pleasant or useful, and now you need him/her/it to be happy. So in one of the most famous sentences in any language, 'I Love You', the word 'I' is so essential in the process of love. But as I explained before, 'I' does not exist. When people lose their memory, all these types of love disappear along with the other aspects of their lives in the world of doing.

Common love can easily disappear, be damaged, or (based on the law of Yin and Yang) be converted to its opposite and become hate. As common love is based on your masks' neediness, it needs constant confirmation to stay strong. That is the reason why very often it is shown off by people, in order for them to prove how popular and loved they are.

It is usually not in your control, which is why people say they 'fell in love'. Common love also needs variety to avoid it getting bored, so time is against it. And as it gets older, it usually becomes more like a habit than a deep emotion. Change becomes necessary to keep up with the need for variety, such as changing your appearance (from hair colour to cosmetic surgery). It requires effort, conversation, and absolutely anything to keep the emotion alive and energetic. If not, it might just fade – which sadly, it does in most cases.

Common love is based on mental taste and physical performance. What does this mean? You probably already have an ideal wife/husband/partner in mind and, when you go to the marketplace, you try to find the closest match to your taste. For example, if you love tall men, you will say yes to the tallest candidate. And obviously, if you find someone taller than him, you should go for the taller one instead. It's the same with other highlights of your taste, from a sense of humour to an education.

Common love is very time- and energy-consuming as it needs lots of maintenance, and that is the main reason some people get tired of it and prefer to live alone. It is attention-based and also related to serving your ego to prove you are worthy of receiving this love and attention. It is based on an on-going competition with other mask providers, and you need to be smart enough to win this game almost every day.

Finally, common love, in the same way as other aspects of your masks, needs a powerful past and future. You get more credit for a longer and healthier past and a good plan for the future than for your feelings now. That is why people celebrate their anniversaries and show off the length of their relationship to other couples. However, most people, based on their own life experiences, can distinguish the difference between love and staying together under the same ceiling.

Real Love

So, what is real love? Most people, generally speaking, are interested in real love – but, of course, in receiving it rather than producing it. A google search of the word 'love' produced 14,650,000,000 sites, and comparatively, 'real love' produced 13,810,000,000. This means that less than 6% of the websites on 'love' were not about real love, but still, the majority of them were directly or indirectly related to it. I will now share with you some of the highlights of my findings of real love and leave the rest to your creativity and curiosity to find out more.

Your soul and mind should be clear from toxins and mature enough to allow the seed of real love to grow in your heart. Those who still identify themselves with their masks won't be able to cultivate the seed of real love. Real love is pure and pious. It cannot survive in a heart that is home to toxins and negativity.

Real love is a decision that you grow into by erasing your ego, and not something that you fall into based on your ego's neediness. Receiving real love is a false desire and delusion as you cannot plan for it, but producing jt is based on your decision. It is exactly the same as cultivating a seed in the soil. After you decide to do it, you need to pay attention to the laws of nature, the same as a smart farmer. When seeds are under the soil, their chance of growing on their own is not that strong. But a wise and intelligent farmer helps the universe by fertilising the soil, watering the seeds, and allowing the sunlight to shine on them. The technology of this process does not belong to the farmer, but he/she can help it effectively and make it happen, and of course, they too will be rewarded by the universe.

One of the very obvious ways of distinguishing real love from common love is by checking the result. In your mind, take two people that you have known for a long time that have been in love and lived together for ten years. Are they much happier, wiser, and calmer now than before? If so, that could be real love. If after ten years they are physically, mentally, and emotionally ill or damaged, and they feel trapped in the relationship, then that this is common love. So, it doesn't matter how many years a couple has been together, but it is important that they feel more space, freedom, and happiness in their hearts – and are more excited about life and people's well-being.

In order to produce real love, you need to clear your heart from the poison of ego and stop mistaking your masks as your real self. You need to fertilise your existence with deep relaxation and allow the light of your being to shine through your masks. Then the magic happens, and the seed of real love (which is alive) starts to grow.

This seed is in everyone and has the potential to grow, but there are a lot of misunderstandings and incorrect usages of the word 'love' created by masks. Temptations, selfish desires, misjudgements, neediness, and confused mental and emotional patterns have been called 'love'.

So what people call love and what they would die to receive is based on their ego, 'I', and neediness. That is why, after a while, their so-called love changes to either the opposite side — hatred and anger

— or it becomes a habit and repeats boring patterns like buying flowers and saying, 'I love you'.

If you manage to become so deeply relaxed that you can reduce the power of 'I', you will increase your capacity to produce love. In the moment that you feel love with no 'I', you realise love and life have the same source. Real love has no 'I' as the operator and subject. When 'I' and 'you' disappear in 'I love you', you are producing real love and are almost ready to experience meditation. Real love will shine to the universe, earth, people, animals, plants, and everything else unlimitedly and unconditionally with no expectation of receiving anything in return, not even an acknowledgement.

Real love is a very reliable bridge between the world of being and the world of doing because the root of it is in your heart behind the masks. Yet it can also be very useful to your masks in helping them play their best in the world of doing.

When you stop identifying yourself with any of your masks, you start to produce real love, which in turn enables you to stop identifying yourself with your masks. If this were the case with everyone, there would be no need to control the power of morality with the law because amazing wisdom comes from this love, which is superior to any other form of control system. But please understand that I am not against applying law and rules or recommending morality. Masks need these control systems to operate in the world of doing and make society a safe place.

In summary, when we talk about common love, it could be affection, infatuation, attachment, or even mutual understanding. In fact, most people nowadays do not even fall in love – they fall in love with the *idea* of being in love. Hence, the presence of neediness. If you look around, people fall out of love the same way they fall in love; but as we've said, the world of doing is a happening place.

Real love falls in between the world of doing and the world of being, and it has a direct connection to meditation. Why? Because real love is eternal. It has no end and no vulnerability. It does not demand or desire. Real love is just there. It just happens, and there is never an opposite feeling for it other than forgiveness. Real love exists and just gives without asking for anything in return. Once it is produced, it cannot be destroyed and it cannot fade. And that, my friend, is the purity of it. Real love activates very important parts and aspects of your existence, and if you are capable of producing it, then you are halfway to meditation.

15

THE NATURAL COURSE OF LIFE

As I've said, the world of doing is quite happening, and everything moves. Whether you look at movement from a spiritual point of view or a scientific point of view, you can see movement by simply observing our internal and external worlds (regardless of your definition).

Take our solar system, for example. The solar system moves inside a galaxy, the earth moves inside the solar system, and we move on the earth. At the same time, we have movements going on inside our body's organs, tissues, cells, molecules, atoms, and electrons. So we find lots of different movement going on inside much bigger fields of movement and so on. The world of doing works with movement on so many levels at different speeds and rhythms – this is called the natural course of life.

Growth, however, is more than just expansion or movement. It has life power. If you asked me about the root of people's suffering at all levels, from physical to mental and emotional, I would say it is because they have stopped growing. People think that after birth, they grow physically and mentally to become an adult and then they stop. That is because all masks are focused on maintaining life, and in so many dimensions and levels, people stop their own process of growth, which causes misery and discomfort. So when you allow yourself to continue growing, meditation will happen to you and help you to grow stronger and in harmony with the natural course of life.

Anyone wise enough to appreciate and respect the way that the natural course of life works on different levels, and works with it, will achieve their goals and find happiness and fulfilment. Whereas those who don't comprehend this powerful aspect of life or disregard it will suffer. For example, if you understand the way your body works with air, food, and water, and you respect it, you will be healthy with a minimum number of superficial illnesses. But if you ignore the way that nature operates on your body, you will suffer and require help from doctors and surgeons.

The natural course of life happens based on the platform of Yin and Yang. Yin and Yang are dynamically interconnected, and not only provide a platform for life to move on, but also explain the way that life is happening at the present moment. When it comes to the natural course of life, you cannot force these two poles of life to move faster, slower, or more towards the Yin side or the Yang side. The circle of Yin and Yang represents balance and harmony with the world of being. Any involvement from you must be based on your understanding of the dynamic movement of Yin and Yang related to what you are doing, with minimum interference, and maximum respect and consideration to the rules of nature. For a long time, this is what has been neglected and ignored in respect of the use of the natural resources on our planet.

Diagram 4

Even the rules of masks are based on the movements of Yin and Yang. Masks always want one side of the Yin and Yang circle, while rejecting or ignoring the other side. For example, people often want more power in their bodies (Yang), but they ignore the need for flexibility (Yin) to be increased at the same time to protect them. By strengthening the body without stretching, they usually get damaged. In society, more power and responsibility (Yang) requires more wisdom and patience (Yin) to match and provide balance.

It is the same for the inner-outer balance of work. The more you want to do outside (Yang) the more you need to prepare inside (Yin). The nature of masks is mostly based on paying attention to the outside world; if something goes wrong, it would be the mask providers or other competitor masks' fault. When there is no matching inner work, obviously, the circle of your life won't be able to grow naturally. It can expand to a certain level, but it will not grow adequately. That is one of the most common root causes of physical, mental, and emotional disorders and diseases.

Over time masks stop growing in order to save energy and try to maintain what they have achieved by using patterns to develop predictions and habits. As you get older, habits become more and more important in your life so that you don't have to think about your actions and reactions, and you can do most things by routine. But the natural course of life is alive, growing, and constantly changing against those habits.

We often evaluate a person by their habits and their power of life maintenance, but the truth is we don't have good or bad habits. Habits are the way we maintain what we have, but consequently they are what makes us numb to the changes in life, and that causes serious problems. People prescribe their eating, drinking, physical movements, posture, taste in art, and way of thinking to their habits, and are very rarely open-minded to new suggestions – even those that are necessary for growth.

So, life in the world of doing grows and moves continuously, and any resistance to its movement causes pain and discomfort. Masks think that it is the movement of life which causes pain, but actually it is the resistance to growth. Fighting the speed and rhythm of the flow of life causes friction and, as a result, disorders and discomfort. You could have the best car engine in the world, but if you tried to run it without oil it wouldn't last long. Similarly, you could be the best swimmer in the world, but if you were trying to swim against the flow of a river you would quickly become tired, weak, and hardly move forward.

So in the world of doing (or the circle of Yin and Yang), everything moves, and one of the most fundamental movements in the natural course of life is creativity based on growth. How does this relate to masks and the preparation for meditation?

Well, in order to prepare yourself for meditation to happen, you not only need to relax, but you also need to be able to grow and feel deeply happy. Based on my understanding after much contemplation and observation, I can say that creativity based on growth is the root of happiness. What does creativity mean in relation to your masks? It means if you are given something bad, you make it good; or if you are given something good, you make it better. Further still, if you can make the better best, you understand natural growth and creativity, and that will give you deep gratification and happiness.

You can use very ordinary masks and perform extraordinary roles on different stages of your daily life. It's the same as creating a wonderful rose with an amazing fragrance just from light, water, and soil. Let's say, people around you are very negative and judgmental. You can use your creativity and natural wisdom to turn the energy into a positive and beautiful feeling and feed it to your heart and others. You can create the masks you need or improve the function of the ones you already have, in harmony with nature, to produce happiness and calmness.

When we talk about creativity, we tend to think about art and design, but we often forget that living life with balance and prosperity is also an art in itself. Once you have acquired the balance of Yin and Yang and found the art in life, meditation is on its way.

16

SOLIDITY AND FLUIDITY

In the world of doing, people see all kinds of density — from solid to gas — in what they call reality. Since your masks are much more familiar with these types of reality, you use the same terminology to explain your mental and emotional relationships with your mask providers. For example, you may describe a stable relationship as a solid one. In contrast, if situations, ideas, or plans are fluid, they are not fixed and are likely to change.

Life in the world of doing is a journey between optimal fluidity and maximum solidity. In the case of the human body, a baby has no strength to sit up but is extremely flexible, and a dead body has maximum rigidity. Your birth certificate does not show your physiological age, as any two 70-year-olds will not be at the same level of vitality. The one with more fluidity, flexibility, and fewer toxins would be physiologically younger and have more harmony between their systems and organs.

Masks tend to make everything more solid and black and white.

Whereas, life performs in all configurations, especially in the fluid and flexible kind. How do you know a tree is still alive? Obviously, you check its flexibility, and it is exactly the same in the field of mental and emotional wellness. One can be very knowledgeable and experienced but wear rigid masks and not be open to any suggestions and changes. This person is more likely to be prone to mental and emotional disorders as they are living closer to death than life.

As far back as you can remember, you know that you were taught by your parents to stand up and walk. You also know that you have been advised by your level 1 mask providers to stand on your own two feet and find the stability you need without help. You have worked very hard in your life to be able to stand up, walk, and even run, and win in the competitions of life. But then one day you get to the sea – maximum fluidity is in front of you. In the beginning, you are afraid of walking into the water because everything you know and have learned about stability becomes unusable. After a few steps of walking into the water, you feel the fear of dying, so you go back to the seashore and watched what other people do.

Most people either sit down in shock or walk to the left or right along the beach until they die, just because they know how to walk. Some people go back and try to teach younger people how to stand up and walk with stability, and never mention the sea at the end of the shore. Very occasionally, you will see one person walk into the water and start to move nonstop until gradually they swim and carry on their journey of life right until the end. These are very rare masters of life who feel meditation and the world of being, and one day these people learn how to fly and disappear from the middle of the sea.

What you do in your journey of life is totally up to you. If you decide to stop identifying yourself with masks and don't take them too seriously, but play the game of life on the stage beautifully (with maximum creativity and flexibility), you will get to the sea and your swimming programme will be activated automatically. You will carry on your journey of life until meditation happens to you, and feel your being behind your masks and fly without any fear or disappointment of wasting your life.

The point is, even if you have been taught almost everything in life, there will always come a time where you will face a new situation. A new situation cannot be handled with old methods – it also requires the evolution of methods and tools. Since the beginning of time, the world has evolved and so have the causes and laws. Similarly, as individuals, we need to be open to developing and changing.

17

EGO SENSITIVITY VS. LIFE SENSITIVITY

W hat is ego? As explained in Chapter 5, ego is the common area between masks in which our inner reporter has a constant conversation with our masks and what we refer to as 'I', 'self', and 'me'. In Chapter 7, I also explained that consciousness with glue is ego. This is the simplest explanation of ego that I have; however, you might find a better explanation of your 'I', 'self', and 'ego' based on your own personal experiences and contemplation.

In the world of doing, your masks face non-stop challenges and competitions from situations, others, and even themselves. When you identify yourself with a mask, depending on how important it is in your life, your intellect and brain start to defend it. Name, age, gender, occupation, nationality, religion, politics, skin colour, and even sports teams create some of the strongest ego-sensitive reactions.

Your inner reporter might evaluate you and decide that you need to be better this year. This is when we hear people say things like, "I need to work on myself" and "I am going to improve my habits". As you can see, all of these ideas and sensitivities are based on duality – one reporter and at least one mask talking about you and making decisions. Based on ego sensitivity, major changes in your life are impossible. Even if you manage to create superficial happiness and calmness, they will be short-lived.

Most of the time your ego postpones plans to sometime in the future: "I will stop smoking next week", "I will start running in the summer", "I will change my diet after Christmas". I have seen so many people read books about ego because their ego was trying to find a way to get rid of their ego and find freedom, and I have heard very strong egos talk proudly about meditating for years when, in my opinion, what they had been doing was actually different forms of relaxation. What masks try to do to improve themselves is as useful as "softening water by using a hammer". A mask can meditate, try to create relaxation, explore the ways of liberation, and even write books about freedom from ego, but it cannot feel the world of being as a mask.

When the gap between reality and your masks' or ego's definition of the ideal is too far apart, you will fall into the gap, known as depression. Ego sensitivity brings down your resilience and causes rigidity in your existence, and as a result you won't be able to make a bridge between the two.

Identifying yourself with your masks causes fear. Fear is the fundamental emotion for masks, and if you mix it with other emotions such as judgment, common love, sympathy, empathy, compassion, anger, or regret it reduces space for you and the people around you. Consequently, your expectations for the future and what might happen also mixes with fear and causes anxiety.

When you stop identifying yourself with your masks and instead feel your existence behind them, your life sensitivity will start to grow. You will feel the world is you, and your life is not separate from the whole of being. You will respond to people, animals, plants, and all of nature with no ego. As life sensitivity increases, your doing will focus more on preparation for meditation and helping and protecting the well-being of others and all features of life as the greatest self. That is the reason that life sensitivity can protect nature, control crime, and foster love and respect in society. Life sensitivity helps keep natural resources clean and creates space for everyone to be happy and fulfilled. Conversely, ego sensitivity is based on separation and causes war, injustice, and crime. It destroys creativity by reducing space and ultimately diminishes happiness and safety.

Life sensitivity and ego sensitivity have a reverse relationship with one another, meaning the less ego sensitivity you have, the more life sensitivity you feel.

18

THE LAW OF STRUCTURE AND FUNCTION

So many problems in the world of doing are based on a huge amount of confusion and misunderstanding of the relationship between 'structure' and 'function'. Everything in the world of doing, regardless of whether it is natural and organic or man-made and mechanical, has a structure and a function.

In the past, for example, when people needed to cut something into smaller pieces (function), they used sharp stones (structure) and gradually learnt to improve the structure in order to improve the function. Later on, when people invented language, they used a noun for structure and verb for function. Nouns are based on the illusion of still images. A lit candle lights a room from the burning of paraffin, but we give it a still picture and a name. This is only useful for the sake of communication and talking about different things; otherwise, they do not exist. But verbs are real – so rain, for example, does not exist; but *raining* does. Rivers do not exist as they are just a constant movement of water, but 'rivering' (an invented word), which is the function of water travelling from the mountains to the seas, exists. The same applies to us: Saied (me) does not exist, but 'Saieding', in terms of all the actions that I do, exists. Therefore your actions exist, but the doer, 'I', 'ego', and 'masks' do not exist. Parenting exists as a very important function of a family, but parents are two people we accept as the imaginary structure.

The discoveries of quantum physics support eastern wisdom and knowledge of the principle that structure does not exist, and it is only the function of energy in different levels that creates the illusion of structure. For the sake of helping masks prepare themselves for meditation and feeling the world of being, we will accept the existence of structure for now, and say that structure consists of some functions together to deliver a bigger function.

So what is the relationship between structure and function, and how does it relate to your normal everyday life? This is one of the most important and useful rules in the world of doing. Structure and function are interrelated, and as is the case with Yin and Yang they complete each other. Whenever the function is the master, and the structure is the servant, everything works naturally and the result is positive. But whenever it is the other way around, and structure becomes the master and function needs to follow it, negativity, misery, failure, and physical and mental illnesses and disorders will be the result. Let's look at a few examples to see how this simple law of nature can change your life.

A pen, be it basic and cheap or expensive and gold, has a structure to keep the ink inside, and the function is for writing. You would never buy an expensive pen if it had no ink or if it could not be used to write with. Similarly, you would not buy an amazing car with no engine because the main function is driving from A to B. If it had no engine, it would have no function, but if you bought this car regardless and didn't care because you loved it, you know where the problem is.

The same rule applies to people's masks. For instance, the structure of a family is based on the masks of a father, mother, son, daughter, brother, and sister, but what is the function? Families function to raise the next generation of healthy, wise, and co-operative members of society, but if they perform their masks with no function that will become the root of so many physical, emotional, mental, and social problems. Another example is your body. The structure is anatomy and the function is physiology. When you exercise, do you aim to improve your appearance or improve your function? Strong muscles look nice, but without an improved function, they are as useful as kidneys with no detoxifying function; the result being rigidity, damage, and death.

Let's consider the relationship between wealth (structure), health, and happiness (function). If your aim for achieving wealth is to afford opportunities which result in happiness and fulfilment so be it, but if a luxurious lifestyle comes at the cost of your health, sooner or later your life will become full of misery and suffering.

Before you do anything with your masks, ask yourself a very simple and clarifying questions: What is their function? Why do I need a new mask? How can I improve the function of my existing masks so that I can keep growing? Is my new mask going to improve people's well-being? If changes in your masks or accepting/creating new ones add to the function of your life (creating contentment and growth) then do it. But if not, it will cause you damage and unhappiness.

How does this relate to your preparation for meditation? If you pay attention to improving the function of your masks and not just defending the structure of them, you will be ready to feel meditation in your life. But if the structure becomes more important than having any major function, you will be more mentally and emotionally confused and potentially physically ill – and this will eventually close the doors to meditation. To feel the world of being, one must be free of toxins and burdens from the world of doing, therefore, I encourage you to use the law of structure and function to find balance and harmony in your life.

19

THE WALL OF LOGIC

What I call 'The Wall of Logic' is whatever masks learn and believe is the foundation of their reasoning from which to analyse and understand their reality.

As explained in Chapter 4, if you draw five lines symbolising your five senses, and they meet one another in a centre point, that circle is the world of doing and the foundation for your wall of logic. That means if you can see something, hear it, touch it, smell it, and probably taste it, you call it a reality. The more your senses are involved in your observation, the stronger your confirmation.

Imagine people were born visually impaired and have never had a sense of vision and have no idea what vision is about. But to go to different places, they have developed a method where one hand always touches a wall, and based on the information they get from the wall, they know where and how to go. Over the years they have experienced, learned, and taught about the materials and conditions of walls – for example, brick, metal, and concrete. Now when they walk with one hand on the wall, they know what kind of wall it is and how they need to work with it and use it as a sign to find their direction. If they touch a new material for the first time, they wait and use an acceptable research method to figure out what is it made of, and write a paper about it to help the next group of people who might touch the same wall. This is the scientific method, and it is a reliable and useful way of building, maintaining, and strengthening the wall of logic.

Then imagine that some people who have one hand on this wall ask you for directions to a place which is on the other side of the road, and you can see this place. As the wall of logic is 2D, they ask you if they need to go to the left or right, and you realise that both directions are equally wrong. No matter if they walk to the left or right, they will get to a traffic light and turn left or right again and eventually end up far from the place they wanted to get to. They might even get to another city, but they won't get to the other side of the road. You cannot give them 3D directions and ask them to stop touching the wall of logic and walk to the other side of the road, because they cannot see. Also, any solution that you would like to suggest must be 2D and not 3D as they will need proof based on dimensions that they can feel and assess. It is as difficult talking about dimensions to a partially-sighted person as it is describing music to a deaf person.

Based on the example, you need to know that masks generally live in the 2D world of black or white, right or wrong. So it is challenging to help masks understand the shortcuts of the 3D world, and it is dangerous for them if you take their hands off the wall of logic as their foundation is based on it.

When you advise people to do certain things in order to improve their well-being, and it doesn't work, the reason for this is that the part of the wall of logic that they touch is different than yours. Obviously, you have your own success story and some other people's accounts of applying your method as your proof of success, but as everyone has their own touch to this wall, the results will be unbelievably different and, in some cases, quite the opposite. Your advice could be based on touching a concrete wall, whereas your audience could be touching a glass wall. If that's the case, the results of listening to you and doing what you asked them to do could be a disaster.

If you advise or help someone with their mental and emotional problems, be very careful and try to figure out what part of the wall of logic they are touching before you share your success story and give them solutions. Your background, your masters and trainers, the books you've written, the followers you have, and the money you have made does not mean your advice is useful for everyone.

If you stop identifying yourself with your masks, attempt deep relaxation, and apply the other techniques that I have discussed, you will be able to feel and analyse your part of the wall of logic. In that moment you are allowing meditation to happen and you will begin to feel the 3D world where you don't need to keep one hand on the wall anymore. Please understand that I have full respect for the wall of logic, but you won't need it for everything in your life if you can see.

20

CHANGE AND ENERGY MANAGEMENT

In the moment that you accept your first mask, your memory starts to work on the foundation of changes on the timeline. Without memory, you cannot understand or analyse changes in your normal daily life or make plans for the future.

Your masks need to deal with these changes daily. In order to evaluate and work with these changes, you need good management. Successful people in different fields are not necessarily the most intelligent, qualified, or experienced, but they are the best managers.

Most people talk about time management but when things don't go to plan they say they "need more time" or "had no time", but in the world of doing, time cannot be extended or reduced for anyone. All people can do is manage their energy level and the way they use their energy resources.

Time is an imaginary platform for memory to perform, and it is the same for everyone. Take, for example, two drivers. Each has one hour to get from point A to point B. One driver goes 50 miles per hour and the other one goes 100 miles per hour. The difference is not in the time they had, but in the cars they drive and their way of driving. Or in other words, the difference is in their management of energy and resources.

Similarly, an ordinary person uses their lifetime dealing with a few of their masks while a spiritual master moves behind the masks and experiences life on different dimensions. The timeline is the same.

Usually, early on in life, people around you will tell you who you are and how you should be by reflecting your masks. Why? Because they need you to play the masks that they have provided you and to carry on playing them so that they have the opportunity to play the mask that you have provided for them. For example, your parents cannot play their parenting mask if you don't play your son or daughter mask. So all of the "you should" and "you should not", "you must" and "you must not" relates to this purpose and carries on for the rest of your life.

Mask management enables you to go to a marketplace and trade some of the masks that you have with other's masks. Evaluating how much energy masks need is key to market trading. You should also consider what level in your life they will belong, and what past and future you believe they have. Lovers often measure each other's love before they love and exchange masks, and it requires a very high level of management to prove the value of your love.

I believe most of the mental and emotional diseases and disorders, and even many physical illnesses, are the result of poor energy management. Obviously, if you use too much energy on one project, the result will be less time and more stress. So the question is how smartly can you evaluate the changes in your masks and the requirements of your mask providers?

All mask providers have different ways of evaluating and recognising your masks and your management skills. A good student gets merit; a brave soldier gets a medal; an exceptional citizen gets a title; each one is rewarded for paying attention to the requirements of their masks. So mask management becomes essential for improving the level of your masks, impressing your mask providers and creating new masks for your projects.

Managing all of the masks, even the stressful ones, becomes a necessity. The level of your management will assess the level of your success. You learn how to play different masks and manage the amount of time and energy allocated to them. If you say your friend is a good man or woman, people want to know what they do and what the quality is of their doing. Your work, marriage, relationship with your parents, your social presence, and everything else in your life requires energy management skills.

It is clear that energy management starts to go to different directions, whereas your being wants you to realise different dimensions, and that happens only with meditation. Smart energy management saves you lots of energy, and that will help you to connect yourself with higher wisdom. When you feel your spirit and the essence of your life in the world of being at that level, you will be able to overcome time and space.

21

THE WORLD OF DOING,
MASKS, AND DEATH

In this chapter, I do not want to examine the idea of death itself, as everyone has their own explanation depending on their upbringing, religion, and personal philosophy. What I want to concentrate on is the relationship between the idea of death and your masks in the world of doing.

The doing part of our lives has a beginning and an end – the same as any other action in this universe. Yes, it is true that choosing a point as the beginning and another point as the end is not standard and is very subjective. But in the world of doing, going on the stage, putting on some masks, and playing some characters in the biggest show on earth called daily life has limited time and space; one day it begins, and one day it finishes. We call these parts of the life performance birth and death, and life is a journey between the two which appears and disappears before people's five senses.

Masks want to live on the stage for as long and as comfortably as they possibly can and are afraid of being taken off the stage by imaginary death. Death is the most negative aspect of life for masks. Other negative circumstances, such as illness and poverty, receive their negativity from death because the closer something is to death, the more negative it is. In contrast, anything that takes your mind off of death such as holiday, drinking alcohol, or medical care is considered to be positive.

It always amazes me when I see masks that are so afraid of death that they do whatever they can to avoid it, but they are actually moving towards it and even inviting it. Masks typically choose the wrong diet and lifestyle, disconnect from nature, count on communication rather than connection, and still want to live forever. When I ask some of my patients to stop drinking, for example, they avoid it by mentioning their need of masks in the form of friends. And similarly, if I ask them to stop smoking, they mention other stressful family or work-related problems as their excuse.

In Chapter 11, I explained that masks are afraid of the idea of death, but not death itself as they have no experience of it. Yet your masks come to you as a package, and all of them somehow relate to the fear of death either for yourself or your mask providers. This is because masks relate to all aspects of your life, including your lifestyle and physical and mental health (as well as your personality, creativity and plans).

If you do not identify yourself with your masks in the world of doing and become aware of your life in the world of being, you will see that death is only the end of playing your masks in the world of doing. Life in a much greater scale carries on from one stage to another, and finishing in one stage does not mean that it has finished completely. If, however, you take your masks too seriously, you will find the idea of death and getting off the stage incredibly frightening, and will try to avoid it at all costs.

Only when you prepare yourself for meditation, and it happens to you, will you feel and know death as a bubble on the surface that is ready to burst and recognize its real life as an ocean. Life (in the form you know) in the world of doing comes with death and is a part of the same circle of Yin and Yang. You cannot have one side without the other. Waking up without remembering how and when you went to sleep is the life side of the circle, and going to sleep and never waking up (in this form) is the death side.

If you do not stop this imaginary thinking about death and the conversation in your mind, you will never ever be able to feel meditation. You can sit for as many years as you want, but your inner reporter will be so affected by fear that it will never allow you to feel your real life in the world of being.

22

WHY DOES DOING 'THE RIGHT THINGS' CREATE THE WRONG RESULT? THE SECRET OF SUCCESS IN THE WORLD OF DOING

The idea of success and failure in the world of doing is completely different for different people, and in some cases, the complete opposite. I do not want to discuss the meaning of real success and failure in my opinion compared to others. Instead, I would like to show you how your masks work with achieving your goals regardless of the nature of your aims and ideas of success.

Many people define success by how much power they have or money they make, and for many others, it is about inventing something or making a difference in people's lives. Whatever your definition is, your masks want to be successful, and nobody wants to fail.

You all know that to succeed, you need to do the right things, in the right way, and at the right time. In the world of doing, your main mask providers have taught you that if you want to succeed in whatever you do, you need to know what, how, where and when to do it. For example, if you want to go on holiday you need to go by plane (what?), book a ticket and pay for it to secure your place (how?), go to the airport (where?) to fly on the right day (when?) and to be at the airport at the right time. The same applies in setting up a new business; you need to know 'what' goods or services you want to produce, 'how' you are going to do it, 'where' the right market is for your business and 'when' the best time is to reach your target audience. You might find other questions like; "who is going to work with you?" or "who are your main competitors?" useful depending on the nature of your business. These are very basic but well-established rules for success in the world of doing and they work for everyone in the same way.

These rules, combined with your personal ability, knowledge, experience and determination, will help you achieve what you want. Those who are smarter, more hardworking, braver and have more financial /emotional support, have advantages over those that don't. So if the rules are the same for everyone, all you need is more of these personal qualities to succeed. This is where professional advisors and motivational speakers can help by providing the right advice and encouragement. However, all these extra accessories put more pressure on you and require more energy, and in so many cases, become the primary source of stress and anxiety.

I am not trying to teach you the techniques and methods of increasing your life accessories, but I would like to address one of the most significant problems people have and share my solution with you.

Based on my observations, most people are surprised and disappointed when they do the right things, in the right way, and at the right time with a huge amount of energy, but the results are not satisfactory and, in some cases, total failures. One of the most confusing examples is when people have a healthy lifestyle: a balanced diet, exercise regularly, sleep well, and don't smoke, drink or take drugs, don't suffer from any congenital/hereditary diseases, are surrounded by love – and they get a serious illness like cancer.

I have seen other people who have started a new business based on proper research and advice: they knew what product was needed, how to produce it and sent it to the market on time with a huge level of determination and motivation. Yet, they lost everything and as a result, became depressed for the rest of their lives.

So what is the answer? I am going to share with you the main secret of success in the world of doing based on my knowledge, experience, and contemplation. I would like to show you a way of doing whatever you want to do and getting better results (regardless of your definition of success) while saving lots of time and energy. So let's see how we can improve the performance and usage of your masks.

Wrong Mask for the Task

Imagine that you are a doctor and proud of your profession, but you do this job not only because you want to help people, but also to make your level 1 mask providers proud. This mask becomes your favourite, and you mainly identify yourself as a doctor as well as a husband/wife or son/daughter, etc. and anywhere you go, in your mind, you are a doctor first performing other masks.

After a while, let's say you want to start a business and invest in producing medical tools. You know what you want to make, you get help from professionals and have done your marketing, but the chance of success in competition with others is very slim. Why? Because your mask is wrong for the task; you are not a businessman. However, if you don't identify yourself as a medical doctor, do your research about successful businessmen, sit down and create a new mask for yourself, and then think and act like a businessman, your chance of success will get much higher. You don't need to spend too much energy and time on your project.

It's the same with your other performances. When you see your spouse, you need to be a lover not a doctor/lover, with your parents a good son/daughter not a doctor/son/daughter, and so on. If you want to do new activities, first you need to find the right mask for that task, and if you don't already have it, you don't need to wait for a provider, as you can produce the right mask for yourself. If you are a medical doctor wearing a police officer's uniform and trying to work in a hospital, you will need lots of time and energy to explain yourself to every single patient and colleague, and still the result would not be the same as wearing a white coat. It is the same inside your mind – if you are not already a successful person, you will never get confirmation from people outside. So in summary, if you wear the wrong mask for the task, you will need lots of energy and accessories to achieve your goals.

Using the Wrong Tools or Using the Right Tools in the Wrong Way

Over the years, many people have come to me for help with relaxation and preparation for meditation. Instead of giving them a complex method and jumping to an advanced level, I have tried to break down the process into very simple steps. To my surprise, they found it too difficult and complicated. When I tried to work out the reasons why, I realised they had either been using the wrong tools, or using the right tools in the wrong way.

Let me give you an example to explain my point more clearly. Imagine I asked someone if they had a screwdriver, a fork, a piano, and a pair of shoes and they answered yes to all of these things. Then, I asked them to go home and do the following tasks for 5 minutes each: loosen and remove a tight screw, eat a small plate of cooked rice, play the piano, and go for a walk and then come back for the next task.

I would expect them to do these things quickly, but to my surprise, they would come back after months and say the tasks were too difficult. "Some of my nails were broken, and still I couldn't loosen a tight screw. It was very hard to eat a plate of cooked rice in 5 hours let alone in 5 minutes, I couldn't play the piano keys for more than 30 seconds, and finally, I couldn't manage to walk for more than 5 seconds." I would ask them to go and try harder because these tasks were simple and designed for beginners. Yet after a few months, they would come back again still not having done them. They would say they asked teachers to help them, and even the teachers (who were more skilled), were not able to do the tasks on the level I had asked.

I decided to go and see why they had struggled with doing these simple tasks and realised they had been trying to loosen the screw with a fork, eat the cooked rice with a screwdriver, play the piano with their toes and walk on their hands.

This is exactly the same story of so many people who have come to me for help with completing simple tasks in their lives like giving up smoking. Instead of asking them to try harder, be braver, or giving them more motivation, I had to correct them by explaining the basic rules of using the tools: 'eat with a fork, loosen a screw with a screwdriver, play the piano with your hands, and walk on your feet.' They immediately managed to complete the tasks with no need for extra effort, learning techniques, practising skills, or spending more time and energy than was required.

Most masks use the wrong tools for the tasks or the right tools in the wrong way or the right tools in the right way but in wrong time and place. The wrong tools for the task are as impractical as the right tools used in the wrong way, time, and place. If you pay attention to these simple rules you will not need a huge amount of willpower, goal-setting, or energy to get what you want. Those who understand these rules will find life so easy while those that don't will struggle and lack energy.

Wrong Direction and Wasting Energy

In the world of doing, directions are so important for masks to avoid becoming disoriented and wasting energy. I have seen so many masks put lots of effort into achieving their goals but in the wrong direction. That not only confuses people, but it also becomes the root of frustration in so many forms and levels. Sometimes you can achieve your goals by using extra energy, but in the end you wonder if it was worth it.

Let's say a friend of yours tells you that whenever he drives his car (especially on the motorway) after five minutes he feels really tired, his blood pressure shoots up, and mentally he feels stressed. You ask him about the quality of his car, and you find out that it is new. Your friend also doesn't show any of these symptoms at other times. After checking his physical and mental health and finding nothing wrong, you decide to go with him and watch him in action. To your horror, you discover that he is driving on the wrong side of the motorway and all of the traffic is coming against him.

There are many people who find everything in their lives is against them: their relationships don't last, they have problems at work, they have misunderstandings with their friends, and their projects produce negative results. Surprisingly, they still blame others around them and try to control the outside world in the way that they want.

My suggestion to them is to stop all of the extra work: judging and controlling others, justifying themselves to their mask providers, and instead staying calm and relaxed and feel the main direction of their life. When they find their main direction, they can then adjust the energy, thoughts, decisions, actions, and reactions of their masks. This saves them a huge amount of energy that can be used in preparation for deep relaxation and meditation. I am not saying that this is an easy task, but it is doable and helps to improve the quality of your life enormously in the world of doing. In Part 2 of *You Are Not Your Masks*, I will explain the techniques that I have found useful for finding the main direction in life and adjusting masks accordingly.

Harmony Between your Masks

You can find and create the right masks, but unless there is harmony between what you have accepted and created, you will still not achieve what you want.

One of my patients, for example, was an artist who wanted to work on a big creative project. She needed a calm and inspiring environment to work in, but she was married to a loud and ambitious businessman who worked from home. Obviously, the disharmony between her two masks as an artist and a wife was the main source of her frustration. She then became pregnant, and the mask of a mother was added to her life equation. Not only did she not achieve her goal as an artist, but she also had a nervous breakdown.

The more harmony you have between your masks, the easier it becomes to achieve your goals and become successful effortlessly. Individually, your masks may be absolutely fine and efficient, but if they are competing or cannot at least work together supportively, they will slow you down and prevent you from achieving your goals.

Emotional Attachments

In the world of doing, masks count on your inner conversation between the reporter and your masks. This conversation is always based on your memory of the past and under pressure, and the influence of your imagination of the future. The result of this conversation is merely thoughts in different depths and speeds. If the thoughts are deep and slow you call them emotions such as fear and anger, and if they are shallow and fast you call them spontaneous thoughts and ideas.

For your tasks, if you have the right masks, the right tools, and the right techniques for using them in the right way, you will be fairly sure about the direction of your life. Furthermore, if you have good harmony between your masks and they support and complete one another; all you need to do is detach yourself from emotions as much as possible. Emotions in any form make you heavy and reduce your power enormously.

For example, if I drew two lines on the floor one metre apart, and asked people to jump over the gap, most would be able to do it successfully. But if this one-metre gap was on the top of a skyscraper, most people would either not do it or jump right into the gap as fear reduces their energy significantly. Another example would be if a child wanted to learn to cycle for the first time with a bike that their recently deceased father had bought for them. The sadness attached to the learning process would make it much more difficult for the child to learn how to ride. The less emotional attachment there is to what your masks want to do, the better and easier the result.

Respecting the Roots of your Masks

Your mask providers are the roots of your masks. If you are not happy with one of your masks, you can either eliminate it from your life, or if that is not possible, you can ignore it and reduce its importance to a minimal level. For instance, if you are not happy as an employee, you can resign and change your job. If you are not happy as the son or daughter of your parents, obviously you cannot erase the connection, but you can reduce it to a minimum in the gentlest way so as not to damage the root. But if you accept a mask and use it to perform on the stage of your life, you have to respect the root, honour your contract with your mask provider, and not do anything against them. Otherwise, your success will not be real and will not give you happiness and fulfilment in the long run.

If you are practising yoga and accept the mask as a yoga student, you need to know that yoga is a system and has spiritual roots. You will not benefit from practising yoga fully if you disrespect its roots. Similarly, if you are practising Tai Chi, you need to respect Taoism as its root; otherwise, you will damage yourself and won't benefit from it.

I am an immigrant and was born twice, once by my parents in the country of my birth and for the second time by myself in England. I came to this country and was given a mask as a member of this society. After accepting it, I used the freedom that I never had before to recreate myself in a way that I had always wanted but had never been allowed. I needed to understand this society the same way as any other nation in the world — its cultural, historical and social roots and its values —and I had to respect them. I did not have to accept the mask as a citizen, but when I did, I benefited from everything in the same way as those who were born here. Now, I have to try my best to express my gratitude and show my respect to its roots, and this is my number one reason for writing this book which I dedicate to my readers.

So whatever you do with your selected masks is up to you, but if you want real happiness in achieving your goal, "do not cut the branch on which you sit!"

Right to be Wrong

The definition of right and wrong is different for everyone and even between masks of the same person. How do you know that something is right or wrong? Obviously, the main source is human nature, but as a child, you have learnt this from your level 1 mask providers. Then as you have developed, you have expanded the meaning and created the foundation of your belief system based on your personal experiences, teachers, friends, and so on. Your judgment about almost everything and everyone relates to the mask in your mind at the time, and everyone has a small private court in their mind to send everyone to, including themselves, for trial.

Since your masks' life and function is based on memory and the past, your personal court always considers all of the evidence from the past. That is the downside of following a culture, religion, or moral code as you won't be able to judge new right or wrong things. For example, visiting friends and family is recommended and praised as correct behaviour in all cultures and countries, but during the Covid-19 pandemic, it became wrong. Some people around the world resisted their government's order of lockdown and to stay at home, and that behaviour cost many people their lives.

As life is so dynamic and everything around us changes all of the time, you need to see the fact that right or wrong should be based on your nature in the present moment and everyone deep down can feel whether something is right or wrong. So if you don't define yourself by your masks, everyone including you and your mask providers has the right to be wrong. As a result, if something goes wrong, you do not need to waste time judging yourself or others – instead, you can try to learn from your mistakes and correct them as soon as possible.

Those masks that only pay attention to wrong things in the past feel depressed, as the time has gone and they cannot change them. Those that worry about the possibility of making mistakes or doing the wrong thing in the future feel anxious. Both depression and anxiety, or the combination of the two, can create the wrong results.

So, regardless of your definition of success, which is very different to different people, one of the easiest and most reliable ways of achieving your goals is learning and using the rules of the masks in the world of doing. By using these rules, you can save yourself lots of energy which can be used towards deep relaxation and preparation for meditation.

23

FREEDOM FROM MASKS

Although I have mentioned the greatness of the world of being, I have to say that the world of doing is magnificent too. If you find that parts of your daily life are painful and uncomfortable, it is because you have not been using the rules of the masks. By contemplating, learning, and experiencing your masks, and experimenting with all of the new rules, you will discover that you can make your life on the stage of the world of doing a pleasant and entertaining place.

You could decide to give up all the masks and live in a cave for the rest of your life, but you would miss out on all of the opportunities for growth in a natural environment, and access to your existence in the world of being. You cannot deny your masks and quit them completely as some of your masks are so subtle and stay with you; even a person who wants to live in seclusion away from society has the mask of a hermit, just as monks have the mask of a monk, master, guru, or spiritual person.

The desire for freedom from masks does not help you to neutralise the pressure you feel and will not help you in any way. When you say that you want to find the way of freedom and get out of the trap of your masks, who inside of you is saying this and wants to get rid of your masks? That is just another mask trying to find a way of eliminating other masks and their influence on your life and real happiness.

You cannot live in a society and reject all of the masks just because you do not want to get involved in the masks' marketplace and would prefer to become a spiritual person. That means you would expect others to take all of the responsibilities of working and providing food, shelter, and security just so that you can carry on with your own ritual.

Real freedom from your masks is not based on resigning from your roles and responsibilities in the world of doing. On the contrary, you can continue to grow by playing your masks masterfully and making your life in this dimension beautiful, fruitful, and full of contentment.

If you understand the rules of working with your masks — their levels, ways of creating and improving them, and eliminating or minimising unwanted ones — then you will not only perform in your life successfully, but you will also find real freedom behind your masks, be ready for meditation to happen, and feel your existence in the world of being.

24

CONCLUSION ON AN INCONCLUSIVE LIFE

Instead of offering you a conclusion on an inconclusive subject, I would prefer to share with you a summary of the highlights of my knowledge and experience that you might find useful in your journey towards enlightenment.

Choosing enlightenment is totally your decision. No aspects or parts of your life are predestined unless you permit others to control your life and make decisions on your behalf. (Obviously, you need to understand the laws of nature, the rules of society and related organisations, and adjust intelligently to avoid any conflict.) But if, for example, you decide to grow a plant from a seed, you need to understand and respect the fact that the growing technology belongs to nature and not to you. You need to put the seed in the soil, water it, and make sure that it gets enough sunlight and really work towards the direction of life power, and then very soon you will see the seed growing.

Your freedom exists in the first step of deciding to grow the seed and using your intelligence to find out about the law of nature and work with it accordingly. As I said, your first decision and working with the law of nature is not predestined, and it totally depends on you. If you do not make the first step, you will not have a plant, but if you start the process and do not pay attention to the law and rules of nature, you will be disappointed and punished by the system, universe, cosmos, God, or whatever you choose to call it, by virtue of not getting the result you expected. Bear in mind the punishment is the negative result of your own action or inaction and not a decision of the universe to do something against you. For instance, if you jumped from a high building with no regard for the law of gravity, you would suffer from pain, broken bones, or even death as a result of your action.

If you believe in destiny, let me tell you from my experience that your freedom from all of the imaginary rules and unnatural influences of your masks (which can affect or destroy your inner happiness and also your chances of finding your happiness) is in your destiny.

If you believe in total freedom, you can create your destiny by voluntarily giving up your selfish freedom and joining the whole wisdom of the cosmos and moving to the direction of life. For example, to achieve freedom in writing about whatever you want, first you have to accept and respect the limited number of letters in the alphabet and the rules of grammar. Similarly, freedom and the laws of nature work together in a very dynamic way (the same as Yin and Yang) to allow you to live your life consciously and choose enjoyment, happiness, and fulfilment.

Let's accept the most common opinion, and say that life in the world of doing is a journey that begins at birth and ends at death as the final destination. If you want to experience deep happiness and fulfilment and never experience physical, mental, and emotional suffering during this journey, then know that in the world of doing, focusing and working on people's well-being is the only road of finding true happiness; the two cannot be divided.

Regardless of your position on this road, your speed, the quality of your vehicle, and the nature of your masks (such as age, gender, nationality, background, religion, education, wealth, health, job, etc.), you will be rewarded by the cosmos with optimum happiness, fulfilment, calmness, and success in all forms. Going to any side roads (for the benefit of 'I', 'me' or 'self') separate from nature's well-being generally, and people's well-being specifically, will result in misery and suffering.

Bear in mind that helping people is not a moral or mental decision one can consider as a mission and act on it. It is a preloaded programme in the core of a human being's nature that is activated when someone needs your help, and you try to respond (legally and morally, of course). For a selfless soul and ego-free consciousness, any personal, social, or global adversity is an opportunity to grow and transform potential vital energy into actual inner wisdom.

The quality and direction of your life are based on your decisions. You can identify yourself with your masks and seek darkness and death or play your masks masterfully and gather enough energy to wake up in the world of being and light. You can decide to imagine yourself separate from the world of being and try to search for a personal or divine purpose if it entertains you. Or you can stop all these imaginary ideas and join the great show of life and allow higher wisdom to take over your intelligence, actions, and reactions. In this way, you will continuously grow, and real happiness and fulfilment will be the very least that you will achieve in your life.

It is totally your choice to face the opposite direction of life (and feel the power of it on your chest like swimming against the flow of a river) or to turn around and allow the power of life to support you at your back. When people feel confused about their lives and ask me for advice, I usually reply by asking them about their choice. Do they want to be trapped in the world of doing where anxiety and depression cause misery, or do they want to become aware of their existence and perform their best on the stage of life and ultimately dissolve into the infinity with optimum happiness?

I would like to share with you one final secret and tell you that this book is alive, and right now at the end of the last chapter, I am genuinely not sure if I have written this book or this book has written the next chapter of my life. However, I am sure that it will continue to grow in the fertile soil of your heart, inner wisdom, and creativity and it will never die in the rigidity of black and white/right and wrong thinking.

Finally, I would like to conclude by thanking you for being with me on this journey and hosting me in your mind by reading this book. I will also leave you with one parting question: in your opinion, what is the best gift that you could possibly give to someone you love? It must be something that is not replicable and gives them space to grow.

If you say love, someone else also can love them. If you say time, energy, attention, or even a unique mask, I believe that others can offer these things also. I have seen only a few people in my life that have managed to produce this gift for someone they loved, and the result was unbelievable; nobody ever could replicate it. I will leave you to use the power of contemplation and relaxation to find your answer, and I will share my findings with you in Part 2 of *You Are Not Your Masks*.

"Your inner wisdom is your blessing."

NOTES FOR READERS

I would suggest that you contemplate and experiment with everything that I have discussed in this book and adjust all parts to suit your needs. Video and audio files for every chapter will be available on our website to provide further clarity.

All feedback, comments, and questions are welcome via email, and I will share responses to popular questions in the form of videos and audio files on our website; private questions will be responded to directly.

Website: www.theineffablegroup.co.uk

Email: info@theineffablegroup.co.uk

Facebook: The Ineffable Group

YouTube: The Ineffable Group

Instagram: @TheIneffableGroup

Twitter: @IneffableGroup

LinkedIn: The Ineffable Group

Printed in Great Britain
by Amazon

76747887R00085